Louis Zimmerman.
Treas.

COMMUNAL SOCIETIES IN AM
AN AMS REPRINT SERIE

HISTORY

OF

THE ZOAR SO

CALVIN T. R
KEARNEY ST
KEARNEY

AMS PRE
NEW YOR

HISTORY

OF

THE ZOAR SOCIETY

FROM ITS COMMENCEMENT TO ITS CONCLUSION

A SOCIOLOGICAL STUDY IN COMMUNISM

By
E. O. RANDALL

THIRD EDITION

COLUMBUS, OHIO
PRESS OF FRED. J. HEER
1904

The Library of Congress Cataloged the AMS Printing of this Title
as Follows:

Randall, Emilius Oviatt, 1850-1919.
    History of the Zoar Society from its
commencement to its conclusion; a
sociological study in communism. 3d ed.
[1st AMS ed.] Columbus, Ohio, Press of
F. J. Heer, 1904. [New York, AMS
Press, 1971]
    105 p. illus. 22 cm.

    1. Society of Separatists of Zoar.
I. Title
HX656 Z8 R2   1971
ISBN 0-404-08467-2   75-134427

Reprinted from the edition of 1904, Columbus
First AMS edition published in 1971
Manufactured in the United States of America

AMS PRESS INC.
NEW YORK, N.Y. 10003

THE ZOAR SOCIETY
ZOAR, OHIO

September 11, 1899.

E. O. RANDALL, Sec'y,
Columbus, Ohio.

Dear Sir: I have carefully read your history of Zoar, and find it the fullest and most accurate yet published and entirely worthy of credence. Your treatment of the subject is fair and impartial.

Yours very truly,

L. ZIMMERMAN,
Sec'y and Treas.

NOTE BY THE AUTHOR

THE monograph herewith published in book form, "The Separatist Society of Zoar," is reprinted, by permission, from the publications of the Ohio State Archaeological and Historical Society. It appeared in the Quarterly for July, 1899, Volume VIII, No. 1. While the "Zoarites" have attracted much attention not only in the United States but even in Europe, especially among the students of history and Sociology, yet so far as known to the writer, no extended account of the Society has heretofore been published. The purpose of the present writer will be accomplished if this contribution to the literature of American Communism proves to be of any value to the student or general reader.

E. O. RANDALL.

Columbus, Ohio, Sept. 11, 1899.

HISTORY

OF

The Zoar Society.

THE SEPARATIST SOCIETY OF ZOAR.

AN EXPERIMENT IN COMMUNISM — FROM ITS COMMENCEMENT TO ITS CONCLUSION.

BY E. O. RANDALL, LL. M., SECRETARY OHIO STATE ARCHÆOLOGICAL AND HISTORICAL SOCIETY.

It is somewhat singular, if indeed not really significant, that just at this time while the views of Edward Bellamy[1] are attracting world-wide attention and receiving an enthusiastic acceptance almost startling in its extent, one of the most complete and perhaps most thoroughly tried applications of the so-

---

[1] Edward Bellamy, born Chicopee Falls, Mass., March 26, 1850; died same place, May 22, 1898. Author of "Looking Backward" (1889) and "Equality" (1897). Editor "The New Nation," established January, 1891. These works advocate a socialistic communism. Bellamy's books reached a sale of hundreds of thousands and some four hundred papers and periodicals have been established devoted to his theories, while thousands of clubs and societies have been formed throughout the country promotive of what is called the Nationalistic Movement, which in certain sections has taken an organized political character, leading to the formation of local, state and national parties. The Nationalistic Movement does not at once demand the adoption of the perfected ideal scheme as described in "Equality," but tends towards an Utopian commune, to be preceded "by the nationalization of industries, including as minor applications of the same principle, the municipalization and state control of localized business."

1

cial scheme of communism has reached a termination and, a self-confessed failure, has passed out of existence, as to its communistic feature, and that too after a duration of more than three quarters of a century, a continuance apparently under the most favorable circumstances.

ORIGIN OF THE SOCIETY.

The history of this communistic experiment is a sociological study, both important and instructive. It is the history of the Separatist Society of Zoar. As religion was the fundamental basis of the organization, the object of its formation, the cause of its emigration to this country, and a prominent element in its operation and final failure, some considerable space is devoted to this component of the Zoar Colony. As is well known to every reader of history, the reformation in Germany in the sixteenth century resulted in the springing up, throughout the fatherland, of innumerable anti-Romish sects. This was especially true in those countries where the union and united oppression of the church and state had become unusually obnoxious and tyrannous. The Kingdom of Württemburg became one of the hotbeds of the revolt against popedom and churchdom, and for three or four centuries before the reformation, Württemburg was noted for the reformatory activity of its people.

While following the leadership of the Wittenberg Monk, Württemburg became, not only the stronghold of Protestantism, but also a prolific breeding ground for countless religious independents, and also for an innumerable variety of sects and creeds. As early as 1544, two years before the death of Luther, a preacher of Waiblingen complained that there were as many sects in Württemburg as there were houses. The Lutheran Church became the church of the state, and the orthodox clergy supported by the compliant government, stood up, of course, resolutely against the dissenting and independent religionists. Among these numerous heterodoxies the Pietists constituted one of the strongest and most influential religious parties— they were hardly an organized sect—but were antagonists to the state church. This sect, or rather theological school, owed its origin and growth to the writings and teachings of Johann Arndt (1555-1621), Johann Andreä (1586-1654) and Frederick Christoph Oetinger (1702-1782). The latter was an enthusiastic disciple of the mystic philosophy of Jacob Boehm (1575-1624). Oetinger's heterodoxy fostered a species of dissent known as Separatism. The Separatists rejected baptism, confirmation and other ordinances. They declined to do military duty or take the legal oath, and refused to remove their hats to their designated superiors—they had no superiors in their own estimation, as all men were equal before the Lord. They would not permit their children to attend the public schools, which were conducted by the Lutheran clergy. Disobedience to the conventional forms of the regular church and the dictates of the ruling state, naturally brought the Separatists into conflict with the government. They were insulted and persecuted. They were brought before the civil authorities and punished with floggings and imprisonment. Their houses and lands and personal property were confiscated; their children were taken from them and sent to orphans' homes or other public institutions. In short, an intolerable and bigoted oppression of the Separatists prevailed, just as two centuries earlier the Puritans of England were persecuted by the Protestant King James.[2] There was

---

[2] The interesting fact should not be lost sight of that while the prime purpose of the expedition of the Mayflower (1620), under the reign of King James I, was for religious liberty, the financial plan and practical working of the Pilgrim Forefather settlement was a phase of communism. The Leyden Emigrants having no means of transportation and being scarce of funds, entered into a hard bargain with one of the English Colonizing Companies of London. "In their arrangements for the voyage, and the business foundation and management of the colony," the Pilgrims formed a communistic co-partnership. The Plymouth Company of London, comprising some seventy merchants, handicraftsmen, etc., "which raised the stock to begin this plantation," had an original capital of some seven thousand pounds, divided into shares of ten pounds each ($50.00). This company was to furnish the Pilgrims transportation and land for settlement. The Pilgrims were to go as planters or pioneers—they were to become stockholders by virtue of their services or contributions. "The shares were ten (10) pounds each. For every person going, the personality (that is, from sixteen years of age) was accounted one share for him and every ten pounds put in by him (in funds or property) was accounted an additional share." This co-part-

no alternative for the Separatists but to suffer or flee the country. They were forced to emigration. The first of these Separatist departures to America was under the leadership of George Rapp, the eloquent weaver-preacher of Iptingen, Württemburg. He first gathered a small congregation in his own house in 1787. He and his followers were duly fined and imprisoned when in 1804 some six hundred of them, mainly mechanics and peasants, landed in Philadelphia and finally located on the Ohio river some twenty miles northwest of Pittsburg, in Beaver county, Penn., where they purchased some five thousand acres of wild land. They called the place of their settlement Economy, and they "formally and solemnly organized themselves into the 'Harmony Society,' agreeing to throw all their possessions into a common fund, to keep thenceforth all things in common; and to labor for the common good of the whole body."[3]

---

nership was for seven years. During this time the Pilgrim colonists were to be supported out of the common colony property. At the end of the seven years, all the possessions of the colony, with everything gained by them, were to be equally divided among the whole of the stockholders—London capitalists as well as Pilgrim colonists. Such was the contract, the essence of which was co-partnership in interest and a communism in support and subsistence. One of the earliest studies, therefore, in this country of the relations of capital and labor is offered in the establishment of the Plymouth colony. In 1623 the colonists raised funds through English friends and bought out the London stockholders in the company, and the Pilgrims thus became possessed of all the stock and property of the company.—[Pilgrim Fathers, G. B. Cheever, page 107.]

[3] The Harmonists or Rappists, as sometimes called, remained in Economy ten years and then moved to New Harmony, Indiana, remaining there till 1824, when they sold their land to Robert Owen, the scientist and philanthropist, author of "New View of Society" and "The Book of the New Moral World." For three years Owen tested his socialistic theories at New Harmony when the experiment became unsuccessful and was abandoned, Owen returning to England, his native country. The Harmonists (1824) returned to Economy, which has ever since been their abiding place. They suffered many vicissitudes, dissensions and desertions. Several times seceders established other communistic societies. The Harmonists at Economy numbered at one time over a thousand members—and in their palmiest days were reported possessed

The company that comprised the Zoar colony departed from Württemburg in April, 1817. A few months earlier several of their number were sent to Antwerp to engage a ship to transport them to America. They chose as their leader one Joseph M. Bäumler, which name was later changed for the sake of English euphony to Bimeler and is so known to-day in Zoar and elsewhere. Bimeler was of humble and obscure peasant origin but a man of unusual ability and independence, a teacher, a natural leader and a fluent speaker. He easily became by common consent the guide and mentor of a large following. There were some three hundred in this pilgrim company. They were from the poorer class of their countrymen. Many were unable to pay their passage, which was provided for by some of their more fortunate companions and material assistance was rendered to these religious emigrants by the sympathizing "Society of Friends," the Quakers of England. The journey of the Separatists lasted some three months, and the voyagers landed in Philadelphia on August 14, 1817. They were kindly received in the City of Brotherly Love by their friends, the Quakers, who provided a large building in which the Separatists could remain until departing for their western home. As further acts of aid by the Quakers, it is related that the "Society of Friends" in England had sent a considerable sum of money to America for the use of the worthy but destitute Württemburgers—a sum amounting to about eighteen dollars for each Separatist. This fund was given the recipients upon their arrival in Philadelphia and was used later to send them on to their destination in the Tuscarawas Valley. As most of these emigrants reached Philadelphia "in an im-

---

of property valued in the millions. They made large real estate investments which proved exceedingly profitable, for the coal mines, oil wells, etc. They built up large industries, shipping their goods throughout the country. The past few years they have rapidly declined. They number now less than a dozen members. Their manufactories are mostly abandoned. Their property has been mainly sold and that remaining has greatly depreciated in value and is more or less encumbered. The society has practically lost its co-operative character and its fate as a communistic society will doubtless be at no distant day that of its kindred at Zoar.

poverished condition," this Quaker beneficence came to them
like an act of Providence and the Separatists have always pre-
served a warm spot in their hearts for the generous and sympathetic Quakers. They tarried in Philadelphia several months,
during which time Bimeler arranged for the Ohio settlement.
He purchased of one Godfrey Haga a tract of five thousand
five hundred acres of land, a military grant in the wilderness
of Tuscarawas county. He was to pay three dollars per acre,
giving fifteen hundred dollars cash —(loaned, it is said, by
their Quaker friends)—and his (Bimeler's) individual notes for
fifteen thousand dollars, secured by a mortgage on the land
for that amount, to be paid in fifteen years, the first three years
to be without interest. This transaction was solely in the
name of Bimeler, but with the understanding that each member of the society should have an interest therein proportionate
to the amount he might contribute to the payment for the land.
Bimeler, with a chosen few of his company, went out to take
possession of this purchase December, 1817, when the first log
hut was erected, others rapidly following, on the site of the
present village of Zoar.[4] The colonists were as fast as possible to cluster their humble homes about this chosen center,
after the custom of the German peasant farmers who settle in a
common locality rather than scatter their dwellings upon their
respective and more or less distant farms.

In the succeeding spring (1818) the colonists then remaining in Philadelphia went on and took up their abode at Zoar
—that is all that were able to do so. Many were too poor
to reach there without assistance and a large number were compelled to take service with neighboring farmers to earn support for themselves and families. They were almost wholly
unskilled workmen and many delayed their journey at an op-

---

[4] Zoar was, as may be surmised, so named from the ancient town
on the shore of the Dead Sea, a city described in Genesis as "a little
one" to which Lot was permitted to take refuge in his flight from
Sodom. The choosing of this name is indicative of the religious character and purpose of the Separatists. They have generally been known
as "Zoarites."

portune station to acquire a knowledge of some useful trade or calling.

This Separatist emigration had been primarily for the purpose of securing religious liberty; secondarily for better opportunities of obtaining a livelihood. They had thus far no intention of forming a communistic society; they held their interests individually, and it was expected that each member should pay for his own share of the land, which had been secured by Bimeler to be subsequently divided and sold among separate purchasers. But the members were unequal in age, strength, experience, energy and enterprise. They soon realized that their individual inequality stood in the way of the collective success of the company. "Having among them a certain number of old and feeble people and many poor who found it difficult to save money to pay for their land, the leading men presently saw that the enterprise would fail unless it was established upon a different foundation; and that necessarily would compel the people to scatter." Early in 1819 the leaders, after consultation, determined that, to succeed, they must establish a community of goods and efforts, and draw into themselves all whom poverty had compelled to take service at a distance. This resolution was laid before the whole society, and after some weeks of discussion was agreed to; and on the 15th of April articles of agreement for a community of goods were signed. There were then about two hundred and twenty-five persons, men, women and children.[5]

These articles of association were dated April 19, 1819, and were signed by fifty-three males and one hundred and four females. The articles created a common unity of interests, present and prospective, whereby all the property of individual members, and their future earnings, should become the common stock of the association, to be taken care of and managed by directors to be elected annually by the members.[6]

---

[5] Nordhoff, Communistic Societies in the United States, page 101.

[6] The articles of association entered into by the society were prefaced by the following preamble: "The undersigned, members of the Society of Separatists of Zoar, have, from a true Christian love towards God and their fellow men, found themselves convinced and induced to unite

In March, 1824, amendatory articles[7] containing features
similar to but more extended than those of 1819, were drawn up
and signed by about sixty males and one hundred females,

themselves according to the Christian Apostolic sense, under the following rules through a communion of property; and they do hereby determine and declare that from the day of this date, the following rules
shall be valid and in effect:"

1. "Each and every member does hereby renounce all and every
right of ownership, of their present and future movable and immovable
property; and leave the same to the disposition of the directors of the
society elected by themselves.

2. "The society elects out of its own members their directors and
managers, who shall conduct the general business transactions, and
exercise the general duties of the society. They therefore take possession
of all the active and passive property of all the members, whose duty
it shall be at the same time to provide for them; and said directors are
further bound to give an account to the society of all their business
transactions."

The other articles relate to the duties of the members of the society,
the adjustment of difficulties which may arise among them, and an
agreement that backsliding members cannot, either for property brought
in, nor for their labor in the society, demand any compensation or restitution, except under the order of a majority of the society.

5 McLean, page 224.

[7] "We, the undersigned, inhabitants of Zoar and its vicinity, etc.,
being fully persuaded and intending to give more full satisfaction to
our consciences, in the fulfillment of the duties of Christianity, and
to plant, establish and confirm the spirit of love as the bond of peace
and union for ourselves and posterity forever, as a safe foundation of
social order, do seek and desire, out of pure Christian love and per-
suasion, to unite our several personal interests, into one common interest, and, if possible, to avoid and prevent law suits and contentions,
or otherwise to settle and arbitrate them, under the following rules, in
order to avoid the disagreeable and costly course of the law, as much
as possible. Therefore, we unite and bind ourselves by and through
the common and social contract under the name and title of "The
Separatist Society of Zoar," and we agree and bind ourselves, and
promise each to the other and all together, that we will strictly hold to,
observe, and support all the following rules and regulations. New
articles, amendments, or alterations, in favor of the above expressed
intentions, to be made with the consent of the members.

"We, the undersigned, members of the second class of the Society
of Separatists, declare, through this first article, the entire renuncia-
tion and resignation of all our property of all and every dimension, form

under which articles, with those of 1819, the affairs of the Society were thereafter managed. On February 6, 1832, the Society was incorporated under the then existing laws of Ohio,

and shape, present and future, movable and immovable, or both, for ourselves and our posterity, with all and every right of ownership, titles, claims and privileges, to the aforesaid Society of Separatists, with the express condition that, from the date of the subscription of each member, such property shall be forever, and consequently also after the death of such member or members, remain the property of the said Separatist Society."

Directors were to be elected by the society, who were authorized to take all the property of the individual members and of the society into their disposition, and to hold and manage the same expressly for the general benefit of the society, according to the prescriptions of the articles. They shall have power to trade, to purchase and to sell, to conclude contracts and dissolve them again, to give orders if all of them agree, with the consent of the cashier, who was to be elected by the society. They were "to appoint agents and to conduct the entire provision of all and every member in boarding, clothing and other necessaries of life, in such proportion as the situation, time, circumstances may require." And the members bound themselves to obey the orders and regulations of the directors and their agents. The children of the members, during their minority, were to be subject to the control of the directors, but without the votes of a majority of the society, they cannot bind apprentices out of the association.

The directors are required to take charge of inheritances of deceased members as universal heirs, in the name of the society; to investigate and settle disputes among the members, an appeal being allowed to a board of arbitrators, which was to be elected and to consist of from one to three persons. The arbitrators were bound to observe the economy of the society, and give orders and instructions, to investigate accounts and plans which may have been made by the directors and their agents. All transactions, exceeding in amount fifty dollars, to be valid, required the sanction of the board of arbitration. This board had also the power to excommunicate arbitrary and refractory members, and to deprive them of all future enjoyments of the society.

New members were to be admitted, being of full age, having been approved of by the directors and board of arbitration, by a vote of two-thirds of the society; and on condition that they should resign all their property to the society, as had been done by the original members. Directors and arbitrators were to be elected as often as shall be deemed necessary by the society. "The highest power shall be and remain forever in the hands and disposition of the society, who reserve the right at pleasure to remove and to establish officers, or to place others in their stead; in short, to make any alteration which may be deemed best."

by the name of "The Society of Separatists of Zoar." This conferred upon the Society the ordinary and usual powers of a corporation, with perpetual succession, with power to hold property, purchase and sell, pass by-laws, etc.[8]

On May 14, 1833, at a meeting of the members of the Society, called in pursuance of said act of incorporation, an organization was effected and a constitution adopted for the government of the Society, under which its affairs have ever since been regulated. All the members under the articles who remained in the Society at the adoption of the constitution, became members of the Society in its corporate capacity.

According to the constitution[9] of the Society adopted under the articles of incorporation (1832), the members were divided into two classes, the novitiates and the full associates. The novitiates were obliged to serve at least one year before admission to the second class and this applied to the children of the members, if on becoming of age they wished to join the Society. The full associates must be of legal age, the males twenty-one and the females eighteen. The members of the first or probationary class did not give up their property. A child of a member or an incoming outsider, wishing to enter the Society, was admitted to the first class if the officials of the Society found no objection. Later on the candidate made application for full membership. The trustees would formally receive this request, inquire into the case as far as seemed necessary, and if no cause to reject was presented, they there-

---

The cashier was bound to keep all the funds of the association, and to apply all moneys which may come to his hands, by the orders of the directors and arbitrators, to the benefit of the society—to pay its debts and to liquidate its general wants."

And it is agreed that individual demands by backsliding members, or such as have been excommunicated, whether such demands may be for goods, or other effects, or for services rendered to the society, are abolished and abrogated by the members themselves and their posterity. These articles are declared to be confirmatory of those of 1819, and extending to a more detailed explanation.

5 McLean Reports, 225.

[8] Vol. 30, Ohio Laws, page 92. (See p. 77 this article.)

[9] This constitution will be found in full on p. 79, etc.

upon would, by posting his name in the public meeting room, give thirty days' notice to the Society of the time and place at which he was to sign the covenant. At the appointed date he would subscribe to the constitution[10] and yield up to the Society any and all property he might then possess. It was not required that he have any property, but he could not be admitted if he were in debt.

Strangers who came to Zoar for admission during the probationary year received food, clothing and lodging, but no payment. During the early years of the Society many friends and relatives of the first comers emigrated from Germany and joined the colony. Very few other foreigners became converts. Occasionally an outsider would enter the community because of marriage to a member. But outside accessions or conversions were exceedingly few. No native American is known to have entered the Society.[11] According to the constitution of the Society, all officers were elected by the whole Society, the women voting as well as the men—all elections being by ballot and a majority vote. The government of the community vested solely in a board of three trustees (or directors) to serve three

---

[10] The covenant the elected subscribed to was as follows: "We, the subscribers, members of the Society of Separatists of the second class, declare hereby that we give all our property, of every kind, not only what we already possess, but what we may hereafter come into possession of by inheritance, gift, or otherwise, real and personal, and all rights, titles, and expectations whatever, both for ourselves and our heirs, to the said society forever, to be and remain, not only during our lives, but after our deaths, the exclusive property of the society. Also we promise and bind ourselves to obey all the commands and orders of the trustees and their subordinates, with the utmost zeal and diligence, without opposition or grumbling; and to devote all our strength, good-will, diligence, and skill, during our whole lives, to the common service of the society and for the satisfaction of its trustees. Also we consign in a similar manner our children, so long as they are minors, to the charge of the trustees, giving these the same rights and powers over them as though they had been formally indentured to them under the laws of the state."

[11] An old member stated that a "Yankee," by which he meant a New Englander, lived with the colony several years, but never became a legal member.

years each, one to be elected annually.[12]   These trustees had unlimited power over the custody and management of the property, and all the temporalities of the Society, but were bound
to provide clothing, board and dwelling for each member, "without respect to person"; and to use all means confided to their
charge for the best interests of the Society.   They had the management of all the industries and affairs of the Society.   They
designated to each member his especial work.   But in this they
consulted the inclination and peculiar abilities of the member,
endeavoring to fit each man into the place for which he was
best adapted.   The trustees appointed the subordinates and su-
perintendents of the different industries and departments of
labor.   This board of trustees, which might be called the administration committee, was accustomed to hold monthly meetings in which foreign and home affairs were considered and trans-
acted.   Beside this ruling board of trustees there was a standing committee or council of five, one member being elected each
year.   This standing committee or council was the supreme ju-
diciary or board of arbitration of the Society.   It was the
high court of appeals in cases of disagreement, dissension
and complaint.   This council had power to excommunicate
arbitrary and refractory members, and to cross out their signatures and deprive them of all participation in the affairs of
the Society.   It was agreed that all disputes should be settled
by arbitration alone and within the Society.   The trustees endeavored to act at all times in harmony with this council.   The
Society elected once in four years a cashier or treasurer,[13] whose
duties were those of secretary and treasurer.   He had sole and
exclusive control of all the moneys of the Society, the trustees being obliged to hand over to his custody all they received.
He kept the books and had immediate oversight over the business transactions of the Society.   There was also an elected
officer known as the Agent General,[14] who acted as the trader
to buy and sell for the Society in its dealings with the outside
world, make and conduct contracts, etc.   The office of Agent

---

[12] See Constitution, Article II.
[13] Article V of the Constitution.
[14] Article III of the Constitution.

General was, when created, regarded as the position of honor and influence in the Society, and to it Joseph Bimeler was elected. It was the one office he held and he continued in it to his death, after which the office always remained vacant. The duties of this office were subsequently performed by the cashier or one of the trustees. The time and place of an election by the Society were made public twenty days beforehand by the trustees and five members were chosen at each election to be managers and judges. The office of president was unknown. The constitution was read in a public and general meeting of the members of the Society, at least once every year, at which time the villagers met and discussed and acted upon their affairs much as was the custom in the New England town meetings. So far as Zoar had any political form of procedure, it was a pure democracy.

THE RELIGION OF THE ZOARITES.

We have already alluded at some length to the religious origin in Württemburg of the Separatists as a sect. We can not properly study the Zoar community without a thorough understanding of their religious faith and practices.

The "Principles of the Separatists," which were set forth in the works of Joseph Bimeler, were evidently framed in Germany. They consisted of twelve articles, as follows:

"I. We believe and confess the Trinity of God; Father, Son and Holy Ghost.

"II. The fall of Adam, and of all mankind, with the loss thereby of the likeness of God in them.

"III. The return through Christ to God, our proper Father.

"IV. The Holy Scriptures as the measure and guide of our lives, and the touchstone of truth and falsehood. All our other principles arise out of these, and rule our conduct in the religious, spiritual, and natural life.

"V. All ceremonies are banished from among us, and we declare them useless and injurious, and this is the chief cause of our Separation.

"VI.   We render to no mortal, honors due to God, as to uncover the head, or to bend the knee.   Also we address every one as 'thou'—*du.*

"VII.   We separate ourselves from all ecclesiastical connections and constitutions, because true Christian life requires no sectarianism, while set forms and ceremonies cause sectarian divisions.

"VIII.   Our marriages are contracted by mutual consent, and before witnesses.   They are then notified to the political authority; and we reject all intervention of priests or preachers.

"IX.   All intercourse of the sexes, except what is necessary to the perpetuation of the species, we hold to be sinful and contrary to the order and command of God.   Complete virginity or entire cessation of sexual commerce is more commendable than marriage.

"X.   We can not send our children into the schools of Babylon (meaning the clerical schools of Germany), where other principles contrary to these are taught.

"XI.   We can not serve the state as soldiers, because a Christian can not murder his enemy, much less his friend.

"XII.   We regard the political government as absolutely necessary to maintain order, and to protect the good and honest and punish the wrong-doers; and no one can prove us to be untrue to the constituted authorities."

Joseph Bimeler was not only their leader and guide to this country, but he was their priest and prophet, if such they had. Bimeler was their spiritual leader and preacher, not by any formal authority, but merely universal acquiescence.   The standard, and indeed the only theological literature of the Zoarites, consists of the works, or rather printed discourses, of Bimeler.[15]   They are in three large octave volumes, the first four parts having the common title:

----

[15] On the subject of the faith of the Zoarites I have made free use of a little German Pamphlet, by Karl Knortz: "Aus der Mappe eines Deutsch-Amerikaners." Bamburg, 1893.   Herr Knortz carefully examined the works of Bimeler and in his pamphlet gives a summary of many of Bimeler's views.

THE TRUE SEPARATION

OR

THE SECOND BIRTH.

SET FORTH IN

BRILLIANT AND EDIFYING CONVENTION SPEECHES

AND

MEDITATIONS.

PERTAINING ESPECIALLY TO THE PRESENT TIME.

HELD IN THE COMMUNITY OF ZOAR IN 1830.

PRINTED IN ZOAR, O., 1856-1860.

These ponderous volumes of theological thought and religious reflection are in German and have never been translated. The original copies are rare; very few Zoar families possess a copy. The last two parts bear the title:

SOMETHING FOR THE HEART

OR

SPIRITUAL CRUMBS

FROM THE TABLE OF THE LORD.

GATHERED

BY A DEVOUT SOUL,

AND COMMUNICATED WITH THE INTENTION OF A BLESSED ONE.

CONSISTING

OF A COLLECTION OF EXCERPTS OF MANY FORCEFUL
SPEECHES AND OBSERVATIONS;

PARTICULARLY DIRECTED TOWARD THE INNER LIFE

PUBLICLY HELD AND READ BY A FRIEND
OF GOD IN TRUTH IN ZOAR.

ESPECIALLY ADAPTED TO THE PRESENT TIME.

PRINTED IN ZOAR, O., 1860-1861.

Besides the history of Bimeler's separation, these works. contain speeches, which the Zoarite teacher made before his people, in a language which was clear and easily understood, although not always correct. According to the testimony of the publisher, they are to be considered as direct manifestations of the Holy Ghost, as Bimeler never studied or committed his utterances. In his opinion, the separation of the people, who had inwardly renounced the world and received Christ into themselves, from the false Christians, was a necessary postulate in the interest of the salvation of the former. In the same manner, it was necessary to declare war on the official clergy, who were called "lazy and useless servants," and of whom it was said, that by their empty, ceremonious trifles they deluded the people and kept them from entering upon the road of truth.

From these speeches, a truth-loving, believing Christian, as well as a true and honest character speaks to us and all living Separatists, who had listened to the sermons of Bimeler, have unanimously declared that he lived up to his teachings. In his speeches, which abound in hints for the practical life, we now and then meet with declarations which would greatly honor a modern progressive theologian. Thus, for instance, he says that the religious needs of mankind are not the same at all times and that, therefore, divine revelation progresses and assumes a character adapted to existing conditions. Bimeler preached from 1817 to 1853, that is, to the year of his death. He did not write his speeches down, and the same would probably never have been printed had it not been that a patient and dutiful youth of Zoar had written them down from his memory at the request of his deaf father, who did not attend the meetings. This work the son performed during the night, as in day-time he had to follow his accustomed occupation. His memoranda embrace the time from 1822 to 1832. In the last mentioned year the reporter died, but happily there was another young man who possessed the necessary clerical skill to save Bimeler's meditations from oblivion. When the founder of Zoar died (1853), there was not a man in the whole colony who could fill his place as speaker. For a time they read to each

FORMER RESIDENCE OF JOSEPH BIMELER.

other from good books, but as is said in the preface to Bimeler's Meditations, by the compiler, "It was not quite so agreeable."

So the Separatists resolved to have Bimeler's speeches printed, that they might be read at their services. They also believed it would be a great sin, if they did not put to the best possible Christian use the good which had been entrusted to them. They therefore purchased a hand-press; and as they found no one in Zoar who knew how to use it, they engaged a practical compositor and a printer, who were charged with superintending the printing of the work. The second publication which was issued from the hand-press of the Separatists at Zoar, is a collection of poems or hymns by Terstegen, the mystic poet of the Reformed Church (1687-1769). Terstegen's collection was used by the Zoarites in their church services. The works of Bimeler and Terstegen were the only productions of the Zoar press. The printing outfit was subsequently sold and removed from the village.

The Zoarites firmly continued in their view, that everlasting happiness could not be attained by outward ceremony, which rather led people astray. Therefore, the Württemburg school teacher, Bimeler, made it his purpose to bring light to the true teachings of Christ and to proclaim them courageously to his followers. As the preface of Bimeler's sermons says: "Christianity must be a thing of the heart. Man must divert himself of his bad qualities and of his passion, and deny his own vicious will and subordinate it to God in order that the old Adam die in him and Christ may arise anew."

The Separatists were fond of designating themselves as those who have found the way that leads to eternal life.

The sermons of Bimeler profess to proclaim true Christianity and their author was considered the mouthpiece of the Holy Ghost. Therefore, it is the latter that speaks in these books and not the founder of Zoar, who is nowhere mentioned. Bimeler used to say, before he commenced his "meeting speech": "When I come here, I generally come empty, without knowing whereof I am going to speak. I first get an inspiration what and of what I am going to speak, but as soon

2

as I commence to speak an infinite field of ideas opens before me, so I can choose where and what I like and what seems to me the most necessary."

In these speeches Bimeler showed how man, after he leaves the state of innocence, starts on the road of nature which leads him to eternal damnation. But, if like the lost son, he turns at the right time and cleanses his heart by penitence, he is again taken into the community of God.

Bimeler is very severe in his treatment of the official preachers, "who enter the pulpit only for the wages and for the comfort of life it affords, and who promote the hypocritical worship and ceremonies, and he reproves them for withholding intentionally from their flocks the true Gospel." He boldly stated the clergy were the pensioners of the state. That they did not get their knowledge from God, but had learned it like a trade in the schools. They explained the letter of the text, but felt not its spirit. They preached for compensation and were given to arrogance and hypocrisy.

Bimeler's speeches contain lessons on morality, temperance, cleanliness, health, housekeeping, etc. As Bimeler possessed a certain amount of medical knowledge, some of his discourses even describe "the inner parts of the human body," in order to show what influence the immoderate use of food and drink may have on them. Bimeler is very liberal towards worldly science and does full justice to its progress. Besides, it is everywhere noticeable that he, unlike most of his colleagues, was an educated, well read and, in many respects, an unprejudiced man. He possessed not only great talent, but a vast fund of knowledge.

For the traditional Christian holidays, he did not have much respect, as he thought one day as sacred as another. Sunday he did not even consider a day of rest, because, as he remarked, the crops sown on that day did just as well as those sown on any other day. If nature makes no distinction in this respect, it was not necessary for man to do so. Time should always be used to the best advantage. The Zoarites worked on Sunday when occasion required, but in late years generally observed the day as one of rest. In spring one should sow, and in summer assist the crops so that the weeds would not out-grow them. In fall, the crops should be gathered, and winter should be used to prepare for the spring work. The lessons of the seasons Bimeler also applied to the spiritual life of man. His parallels in this respect are distinguished from other sim-ilar teachings by their wealth of original and practical thought.

His speeches, however, lack logical construction. "The most heterogeneous subjects are often thrown together higgledy-pig-gledy, which is especially annoying, because there is no connecting thread. But this fault may be chargeable to the amanuensis who certainly was not a stenographer."[16]

The Separatists of Bimeler's school, like most other Separa-tists, were inclined to chiliasm.[17] In course of time, however, they came to the conclusion, that the kingdom of God would not come outwardly, but inwardly, and even then slowly and by degrees. A state of grace could only be gradually attained by sincere re-pentance; just as a person could not exchange his sick body for a sound body by legerdemain. A new heaven and a new earth can be created only, if by the killing of the old Adam we ourselves become new. If the latter is not done, a new heaven or earth are of no use to us.

But Bimeler does not put all the blame on old Adam, for he believes that all men have a desire to taste of the tree of knowl-edge. Adam consequently acted simply according to human na-ture. He was just like men nowadays and had his bad and good qualities, the same as they are found in all other products of na-ture, such as plants, animals and minerals.

Nor does Bimeler think much of foreign missionary work, because, he thinks, it is much more important for a true Christian to do this missionary work at home. The professional mission-aries only make nominal Christians and hypocrites, who may be able to recite the confession of faith, but otherwise know as little of Christ's plan of salvation, as they do of the man in the moon.

In regard to marriage, which is always a vexed question in

---

[16] Karl Knortz.

[17] The doctrine that Christ will reign on earth a thousand years visibly and personally before the end of the world.

the confession of faith of the separatists, Bimeler does not always express himself as clearly and distinctly as he really intends. But this much is sure, he did not consider the married state absolutely sinful, as he himself was married and the father of several children. He said he knew, that many believed him opposed to marriage, but added, that if it enhanced the happiness of people, he had nothing against it. Moreover, such happiness was only temporary and ended with death. But he wished that the endeavor of men was principally directed towards acquisition of eternal happiness. A chaste life is therefore preferable, because through marriage sin with all its sad consequences is perpetuated. The married state could only in very rare cases be called sacred.[18]

Many of the members of the original company were opposed to the institution of marriage and decided to make celibacy obligatory in the society as had Rapp with the Harmonists. Bimeler himself at first supported this view and taught that God did not look with pleasure on marriage, but that He only tolerated it; that in the future world there would be no marrying or giving in marriage; that "husband and wife and children would not know each other" in heaven as there was no distinction of sex there. For the first ten years of the society therefore Bimeler opposed marriage and it was prohibited until about 1828 or 1830, when Bimeler was smitten with the charms of one of the comely maidens who was an inmate of his household and whose duty it was to wait upon the spiritual and temporal head of the Society. They were married and this wedding and example of the leader led to the abrogation of the anti-marriage rule and the previous celibate practice of the Society. The benedict Bimeler, consistent with his new and happy state, then freely advocated marriage as shown by his discourses.

With regard to education, Bimeler says many things that deserve notice. As a good example is much more efficacious than words, he exhorts parents to lead an exemplary life, whereby they can influence their children better than by the everlasting admonition to pray and to attend prayer meetings, which fills them only with abhorence for the Word of God. Prayers at stated hours

---

[18] Karl Knortz.

do not at all promote the fear of God, because, if one is not in the right humor, they are easily regarded as a troublesome function. Prayers must be short. Long prayers are an abomination. Bimeler himself did not pray, at least not outwardly, but inwardly, "in spirit and in truth." All prayers must come from the heart, free and unforced. Therefore prayer books are not only unnecessary but injurious to the true Christian, because they "promote babbling with the mouth." Bimeler sincerely appreciated the freedom, which obtained in American school and educational matters, and the fact that there was no attempt made to prejudice the young mind against any social or religious tendencies. The youth are permitted to attain their majority, when they may choose for themselves. This is entirely in harmony with the divine intention, according to which men are created free and which does not favor any creed that may have been created, parrot-like, during infancy. Bimeler was a decided admirer of the republican principle of government and he demanded what was perfectly in harmony with it, the subordination of the individual will to that of the whole, as otherwise in a community like Zoar peace and harmony might be easily disturbed.

As all strife of the world may be traced back to selfishness, man must restrain love of self in the interest of all which, however, few will try and fewer still achieve. But it is said, "Love God with all thy heart and thy neighbor as thyself," and the latter is only possible through restraint of self-love, which, therefore, is a divine commandment. It is easy to love God, it is harder to love one's neighbor. But as men are one family the individual has no right to refuse to love his neighbor. The Separatists therefore took as their model the first Christian community of Jerusalem, where all were one heart and one soul. There was no compulsion there. But as soon as Christianity adopted compulsory means for its preservation, it began to decay. In a communistic colony there are neither poor nor rich. In the outer world there is wealth, and poverty, of which Bimeler prefers the former, because in its proper application it may conduce to much happiness, while the latter often produces many sins and much misery.

Bimeler nowhere appears as a zealot or fanatic and with the exception of the clergymen, whom he thoroughly hates, he condemns nobody, because we only see the acts of men, but not their motives. Nor is he an admirer of blind superstition; and wherever there is a chance, he praises the advance of science, because it improves the condition of everybody. Every new invention he hails with sincere joy. He always speaks like a loving father to his beloved children. He never acted toward his people in a tyrannical manner as Father Rapp (of the Harmonists); he exhorted but did not punish, and if some one differed with him, Bimeler did not for that reason expel him from the community.

Like Father Rapp, Bimeler had declared war on tobacco, without, however, entirely prohibiting its use; as he never demanded servile obedience, which would suppress individual views. Everybody should reflect for himself on all questions of life and form his own independent opinion. Therefore he says:

"We must be glad, that God has led us out of our former fatherland, which is kept so much under pressure and servitude. We should rejoice and thank God with all our heart, that He has freed us from that servitude, and brought us hither, where we can serve our God without hindrance and molestation, according to our conviction and conscience. You know, my friends, in Germany they did not allow us to do so, and therefore we had no other choice but leave the country and seek a livelihood somewhere else. This was the reason why we came to America. It was not selfishness, nor greed, nor avarice, nor desire for any easy life, that caused us to emigrate. No, no such base motives led us to this step. If either of these had been our motives, as is the case with thousands of emigrants, we would not be so peaceful and satisfied within ourselves, as we indeed are, because we know that our motives were, as above mentioned, a desire of a free practice of our principles. And I do not believe, my friends, that we should have attained our aim, if we had been guided by those ignoble intentions."

The old piety which was cultivated by Bimeler and his original followers had to give place in Zoar to ideas more adapted to the present world. But in spite of all that, the Separatists of the third generation until recently (as stated by Herr Knortz) still sang the favorite verses of the old Separatists, one of which verses was:

Yearning is the soul in me
  After peace,
That my troubles, stilled by Thee,
  Soon may cease.
Lead me, Father, out of harm,
To the quiet Zoar farm,
  If it be Thy will.

LEGAL STATUS OF THE SOCIETY.

Much speculation at various times was indulged in concerning the legal status of this society; its character as an organization and the legal relationship of its members to the Society. In several instances the courts were called upon to consider these questions. Members who were deprived of supposed rights, or who had been expelled, at different periods. in the history of the society, resorted to the law for remedy. Two of these cases became famous and important as legal precedents. In the April Term, 1851, a suit was brought by John G. Gösele and others in the Seventh Circuit Court of the United States.[19]

John Gösele was one of the original Separatist emigrants. and continued as a member of the Zoar community until his death in 1827. He was a subscriber to the association articles of 1819 and 1824, but died before its incorporation. His heirs, John G. Gösele and others, brought this suit for a partition of the Zoar property and the restitution to them of their ancestor's distributive share. This raised the question of the nature of the contract entered into by the members and also the character of the organization under our laws. Did the Society constitute a joint tenancy or a perpetuity in property, both of which our laws forbid? If such was the contract it should be declared null and void. Or was the scheme some legal form of a partnership, and if so, did the death or withdrawal of a member destroy this partnership, and compel or permit the distribution of the co-partnership property. And how did the laws governing real estate descent apply to the lands of the community?

---

[19] John G. Goesele et al. vs. Joseph M. Bimeler et al., 5 McLean Reports, 223.

"The rights of the plaintiffs in this suit rested upon the contracts before the incorporation of 1832. They claimed: 1, that there was no grantee (of the lands); 2, that if there were a grantee, the grant would be void as a perpetuity. To this the court, in its opinion, replied that the lands were purchased by Bimeler for the Society, were paid for by it, and were held in trust by him; the fee was in him and the members of the Society were the *cestui que trusts*. It was admitted that an unincorporated community could not, in its aggregate capacity, take lands in grant, nor could its directors and their successors in office take them, as the law, under the circumstances, recognizes no succession. A valid grant to such a community would only be made to the individuals composing it, or to an individual and his heirs, in trust for its use. The articles of association constituted a declaration of trust, which Bimeler, the trustee, recognized as binding upon him. This declaration did not require the formalities of a grant; it was in writing and the application of the trust being distinctly stated, it was not affected by the statute of frauds and perjuries. The members of the Society agree with each other that their property of every description should be held and used as a common fund for their general benefit and they appointed certain agents to manage their concerns and provide for their support. It is true, they relinquished to the Society their entire property, but it was done that, as a community, they might enjoy the benefits of the whole. The aggression which they established relieved the members generally from personal care, but the sum of their enjoyment was not lessened. The want of capacity in the Society, as deeds to take by grant, does not invalidate this procedure. The agreement was that the equitable individual right to the trust should be relinquished for a common right with the other members, to the entire property. In effect, it was constituting a universal partnership, known to the common law and which is not in violation of any of its principles, the name of the Society was used as a designation of the whole body, the same as the assumed name of a firm to designate its partners. Individuality of membership of **the property then possessed by the members of the association** was abolished, and also future acquisitions for the common right of an interest in the whole. This common right was limited to the members of the association; consequently those who left it, or were expelled, forfeited such right. * * * * By this arrangement, the members of the association were placed on an equality as to their interests in the property and their enjoyment of it. Their minutest wants were alike provided for, through the agency established; and this was the consideration on which the contract was founded. That, in the absence of all fraud and unfairness, this was a bona fide and legal contract, cannot be doubted. An important part of this contract was that the property thus surrendered should belong only to the members of the association; consequently the heirs of the members could not claim an interest in the property as heirs, but only as members. Against such a disposition of property, I know of no principle of law or morals. Any individual has the power to divest himself of his property, real and personal, for a valuable consideration.

"Gösele and the other members, when they relinquished their individual property for a common interest in the whole, and appointed agents to manage the concern, expressly agreed to receive as a consideration for their property and labor a support for themselves and their families, including clothing and every other provision necessary for their comfort. * * * * It was a partnership agreement among themselves, and was binding upon each individual who entered into it.

"If there be no principle of law opposed to such a community of property, it must be held valid on the rules which apply to partnerships. There was no moral considerations opposed to it. In adopting it, the Separatists Society followed the example found in the early history of the Apostles, and which received a lawful sanction of heaven.

"But it is said that this association contemplates an enjoyment of the property in perpetuity; that those who shall become members of it, through all time shall enjoy it, and that this the law will not permit. * * * * It must be observed that title (to the land) vested in the trustees from the date of the deed; and the common use, in the society, as fully when the articles were agreed to, as was contemplated at any future period. It is true that the association could only be perpetuated by the admission of new members. But such admission is not obligatory on the Society. An applicant to become a member must first apply to the directors, who bring his case before the board of arbitration, and pass their examination. If admitted, it must be on the condition that he shall relinquish his individual property to the members of the association, and with them enjoy a common benefit in the whole. This is a matter of contract at the time, as it was at the formation of the society. The perpetuity then, is not created by the first contract, but depends upon subsequent contracts, which may or may not be entered into. No right is derived or can be claimed under the articles of association until the individual shall have complied with the conditions of his admission. He then becomes a partner in the association, and is subject to the original articles, not from any instrinsic force in them, but because he has adopted them by contract. Here is the origin of his right, and of his obligation, and the question may well be asked, is this a perpetuity? If it be a perpetuity, it is a perpetuity that can extend beyond lives in being, only by voluntary contracts. * * * * This association, in principle, does not differ from any other partnership, where the members create the capital by giving up their property to the concern, living upon their profits, applying their surplus to an increase of capital, and receiving new members on the terms of the original association. This, if carried out, may endure for many generations, but it is not a perpetuity, which the law prohibits. The enjoyment of the right, on condition of continued membership, has no necessary connection with a perpetuity. If the condition be broken by a member, it depends upon the individuals and the Society whether he shall be restored or not. * * * * For the reasons stated, I think the agreement entered into by the members giving up their individual interest in the property for a common interest in the whole of it, so long as they shall remain members, is not void in law."

The federal circuit court decided the case for the Society

and against the contestants. They appealed the case to the United States Supreme Court, when it was tried in the December term, 1852, Roger B. Taney being then Chief Justice. The interests of the Society were defended by no less distinguished advocates than Henry M. Stanberry and Thomas Ewing. Mr. Stanberry, in a very learned brief, argued that the association was not a simple pure partnership, liable to the incidents of such and subject to the operation of all the ordinary causes of dissolution—viz: that it might be dissolved by the first death which happened among its members, and was capable of dissolution and partition of its real estate, at any time at the instance of any member. "The original agreement provides," he said, "for a perfect community of property, real and personal, and for a succession or survivorship among members on the Tontine principle. It guards with great care against the dissolution of the body. * * * This was not a mere partnership, nor the members tenants in common. The agreement for community of property, the mutual surrender of all individual property into the common stock and the express stipulation against any reclamation in the case of withdrawal, and for the preservation of the common property, for the exclusive use and perpetual enjoyment of the members, in succession, are inconsistent with the incidents of mere partnership or tenancy in common.

"But, is is said, there are legal difficulties which the agreement of the parties cannot surmount. That upon the death of a member, the Society was dissolved *ex necessitate.* This consequence, though generally true as to partnerships, does not follow where the agreement provides against it. It is not an inevitable consequence. The doctrine of dissolution upon the death of a partner, only obtains where the deceased partner has a continuing interest in the property or profits of the association. It is not just that the surviving partners should be obliged to carry on the business, without his co-operation, for the benefit of his estate.

"I have said this Society was not an ordinary partnership, It very closely resembles that sort of partnership in the civil law which is called universal. "Universal partnerships (*des so-*

cieties universelles) are contract by which the parties agree to make a common stock of **all** property they respectively possess—they may extend it to all property, real or personal, or restrict it to the personal only. They may, as in other partnerships, agree that the property itself shall be common stock, or that the fruits only shall be such; but property which may accrue to one of the parties, after entering into the partnership, by donation, succession, or legacy, does not become common stock, and any stipulation to that effect, previous to the obtaining of the property aforesaid, is void.'

" 'An universal partnership of profits includes all the gains that may be made, from whatever source, whether from property or industry, with the restriction contained in the last article, and subject to all legal stipulations between the parties.'
* * * This association is a general partnership, with the principle of survivorship ingrafted upon it. In this particular it takes the character of a Tontine, which is a society with the benefit of survivorship, the longest liver taking the common property in absolute ownership. * * * * I can see no objection to this provision as to ownership. Certainly as to personalty there can be no difficulty; but it is said, in so far as the real property of the company is concerned, there can be no joint tenancy, no right of survivorship, in Ohio; and that upon a death of a member, his interest in the real estate passes to his heirs at law, and that at any time the right to partition might be asserted. * * * * There is, then, no objection to survivorship by express limitation or agreement. This being so, there has been no descent of any heirs of the deceased members of the society, and there is no present right of partition in any of the living members.

"Objection is also made to this association, that the principle of community and succession of property among the members, involves a *perpetuity*. There is nothing like a perpetuity in it. The society has the perfect right of disposal over all its property, real as well as personal, and this power of disposal is wholly inconsistent with the idea of perpetuity, which only exists where the property is so limited that no living agency can unfetter it.

"It is further urged that this Society is contrary to the genius of our free institutions—that its constitution enforces perpetual service and adherence to a particular faith, and that it is aristocratic in its tendency.

"If there were anything in such objections, the constitution answers them all. So far from being at all aristocratic, this Society is a pure democracy. All the officers are chosen by ballot, every member, male and female, have an equal voice; and the body of the Society reserves to itself the power of removing officers and changing the form of government at pleasure. All distinctions of rank or wealth are abolished, and a perfect equality provided for. No single dogma in religion or politics is announced, no unusual restraint on marriage, nor subserviency to any doctrine out of the common way, exist; and so far from any enforcement of perpetual service being provided for, the right is reserved for every member to retire from the society at pleasure, with the single condition that no claim is to be set up for services or property contributed. The powers which the Society confides to its officers are temporary, and so distributed as to prevent any one member or officer from engrossing too much power.

"Besides this liberal frame of government, the constitution, by very full enactments, provides for the education of the children, the comfort and support of all the members, and the peaceable settlement of all controversies by domestic tribunals. It is impossible to hold that such a constitution is contrary to public policy, or in any sense illegal. To say that such a society cannot exist under our form of government is a libel on our free institutions.

"This is not a perpetuity in the common law sense of the term, it does not tie up real estate, for it may be disposed of at any time. Such a limitation of the real estate, or its proceeds, would be good, by the laws of Ohio, for the lives in being; and each tenant for life, by his own signature, if the full estate at any time vested in him or them, could equally well transmit it to another life, and so in succession, a majority being at all times able to terminate the succession at pleasure."

Justice McLean delivered the opinion of the court in which

he said that "according to the plan of the Zoar articles that Gösele renounced individual ownership of the property and an agreement was made to labor for the community in common with others, for their comfortable maintenance. All individual right of property became merged in the general right of the association. He had no individual right and could transmit none to his heirs. It is strange that the complainants should ask a partition through their ancestor, when by the terms of his contract, he could have no divisible interest. They who now enjoy the property enjoy it under his express contract. * * * * This was a benevolent scheme and from its character might properly be denominated a charity. But from the nature of the association and the objects to be obtained, it is clear the individual members could have no rights to the property except its use, under the restrictions imposed by the articles. The whole policy of the association was founded on a principle which excluded individual ownership. Such an ownership would defeat the great object in view, by necessarily giving to the association a temporary character. If the interests of its members could be transferred, or pass by descent, the maintenance of the community would be impossible. In the natural course of things the ownership of the property in a few years, by transfer and descent, would pass out of the community into the hands of strangers, and thereby defeat the object in view. By disclaiming all individual ownership of the property acquired by their labor, for the benefits secured by the articles, the members give durability to the fund accumulated, and to the benevolent purposes to which it is applied. No legal objection is perceived to such a partnership. If members separate themselves from the Society their interest in the property ceases, and new members that may be admitted, under the articles, enjoy the advantages common to all."

A subsequent suit[20] was begun in the common pleas court of Tuscarawas county, carried through the circuit court and finally decided in the Ohio supreme court in the December term, 1862. That case was brought by John Gasely and his wife Anna Maria Gasely. Anna Maria, with her father, was one of the emigrants

---

[20] Gaselys et al. vs. Separatists' Society of Zoar et al., 13 Ohio State, 144.

of 1817, John Gasely was also a member. They were married in 1830 and signed the articles in 1833. In 1845 John Gasely was expelled from the Society, "for just and sufficient cause," it is claimed, and his wife, Anna Maria, "was compelled to leave also or abandon him and their children, which she was unwilling to do." The petition of the Gasely's was for their distributive share of the Zoar property. In this case also the Supreme Court of Ohio sustained the contract upon which the community was based.

PRACTICAL WORKINGS OF THE SOCIETY.

The location of the settlement of Zoar was well chosen on the east bank of the Tuscarawas river, in the northern part of the county (Tuscarawas) where the stream flows through a valley fertile in soil and rich in scenery. The Ohio and Erie canal[21] passes near by and the town is a station on the Wheeling & Lake Erie Railroad. Alighting from the train one seems to have left the modern American civilization and to have suddenly dropped into a little German village that dates its origin to a century or more ago. One of the county highways passes through it and forms its principal thoroughfare called Main street, and the only one having a name — and running almost due north and south. The village consists of not more than seventy-five buildings — of various shapes and sizes — and scattered irregularly upon eight or nine streets, two of which on either side are parallel to Main, the other four crossing these at right angles and extending east and west. Excepting Main, the streets are narrow and unimproved, there being no curbs or gutters, and on the side streets no distinctive walks unless created by packed ashes or gravel, making a footway slightly raised above the level of the road. There was no system of sewage or drainage — though water was brought into the village by piping from a spring on the hill north of the urban limits; water was thus conveyed to one or two public drinking troughs, but it was generally not carried into the houses. Zoar seemed to studiously avoid modern conveniences. Particularly did it shun light; at some of the street corners a wooden

---

[21] The Ohio and Erie Canal was built 1825–1833 and extends from Portsmouth to Cleveland.

lamp post stood like a lonely and almost useless sentry, as the apparatus for illumination was either wanting or impaired. But there would seem to be little or no need of village lights as the good people had rare occasion to "go out o' nights." The streets, however, were cleanly; the village for the most part had a trim and swept appearance, characteristic of the German habit. The garbage of the dwellings was gathered each day in a wagon and carried off. The home interiors were scrupulously scrubbed and dusted. The total population did not exceed 300 including the Zoarites proper and the employed help. The natives lived in some forty dwellings — a fewer number than usually obtains in a settlement of an equal number of inhabitants. Many of the domiciles were double and accommodated two or possibly three families. The other buildings were for public or common purposes, — factories, barns, store-houses, hotel, town hall, church, schoolhouse, etc. The living houses were of various ages and styles — antiquity prevailing. Some of the log cabins still stood in part— if not entire — mementoes of the pioneer life of the Society. The later frame structures were a story, a story and a half, in a few instances, two stories high. There were a few old time red bricks with heavy beam lintels. These homes though indicating the strictest economy in construction and form were comfortable; the rooms were usually large, square and low, the windows often placed high up and small; the chimnies were often those of "ye olden tyme." There were no cellars and no garrets. The floors were mostly bare or partially and cheaply carpeted. The furniture was simple, sparse, heavy and time-honored. Pictures and ornaments were few and far between. A rigid plainness existed throughout these humble homes, nor was there any variation denoting different degrees of comfort or means as one sees in every other village. There was an undeviating sameness in the mode of living.

The houses stood close to the street, upon which the steps often projected, but in nearly every instance an extent of yard surrounded the house on the sides and rear. These yards were invariably utilized as vegetable and flower gardens. Each family mainly raised its own vegetables though the more common ones were supplied by the Society. Flowers in great profusion was

OLD AND NEW HOTEL.

the one and almost the only æsthetic feature of Zoar domesticity. But the flowers were mostly the old fashioned sort. "Roses red and Violets blue, and the sweetest flowers that in the forest grew." In some cases the homely walls of the antique homes and the lattice of the open porches which many had, were decorated with climbing foliage and creeping flowers. Their devotion to floriculture was evidenced by public recognition, in the maintenance of a flower garden or park situated in the center of the village, facing on the main street and occupying a full square, an acre or more of ground. In the midst of this space was an arbor uniquely devised by spruce trees so planted and trimmed as to form a tree cabin, in which were wooden seats — offering a most suitable trysting place for the Zoar Romeos and Juliets. From this bower, so curiously combining art and nature there radiated, like spokes from a hub a series of narrow walks flanked with beds of blossoms and rows of small shrubbery. This garden was the special pride and pleasure of the villagers and from time memorial has been cared for by some member especially delegated as the gardener. It has been the admiration of all visitors and the subject for many an artist.

The other picturesque characteristic of the village were the old, red, heavy, trough-shaped, tile roofs that covered many of the buildings. At one time the manufacture of these tiles was an industry of the Society, but long since the market for these obsolete goods ceased.

Near the garden, lofty stone steps ascending to the entrance, was the conspicuous dwelling of the village — the former residence of the leader, Joseph Bimeler. This edifice, often designated by the visitors as "the palace," was a spacious basement and two and a half story, cupola surmounted, red brick mansion; a two story, colonial columned portico extended the full width of the front. It was erected in 1835, a few years after the marriage of the founder of the Society — in those days a most costly and pretentious establishment and certainly not only far beyond anything in its locality, but quite equal to the best western manorial homes of its age and generation. This semi-official residence was given a somewhat villa like appearance by the ample grounds on

3

either side, in which flowers and small fruit flourished in great profusion. The interior arrangement was in accord with the striking exterior architecture. Here Bimeler lived until his death in 1853. Bimeler taught equality of life and in his discourses played the part of a "great commoner," but this comparatively aristocratic abode — so far in excess of anything any of his associates occupied — rather suggests the suspicion that the disciple of democratic commonality was not averse, even at the expense of the community, to enjoying some exclusive luxuries. At times, however, this conduced to criticism and even open charges, particularly from those who withdrew or were driven from the Society. It was claimed by the Gösele contestants that Bimeler was making a good thing out of his prominent position and that the Agent-General traveled about in "a gay and brilliant equipage that flashed and spun," consisting of a fine carriage and span of speeders. This imputation was not sustained and it was proven in the trial that the carriage was a very ordinary one, "worth only about three hundred dollars," that one of the horses cost about twenty dollars and the other thirty or forty dollars. It was unmistakeable however that Bimeler did ride about with his wife — while his equals footed it. But it is also true in extenuation of this privilege—unenjoyed by other Zoarites—that he was permanently lamed by a broken leg, his carriage conveyance being necessary. But beyond doubt Bimeler seasoned his plain thinking and simple teaching with no slight flavor of high living, but that seems to have been willingly and cheerfully allowed by his contemporary people. Undisputed tradition and the universal testimony of the aged members, still living, who remember Bimeler, deprecate any aspersion upon the character, morality, honesty or sincerity of precept or practice of their founder and acknowledged superior. With just cause they all respect and honor his memory as an able, just and true man — devoted to the welfare of his fellow-members. This official residence for the past few years has been used in part as living quarters for some of the families and in part as the storehouse or repository for the goods to be distributed to the members, groceries, clothing and living necessities. To this building on (two) designated days of the week the villagers would go to procure their supplies — each family being allowed ample quantity, of the articles supplied, both food and such things as were fur-nished for the housekeeping. No account or reckoning of this distribution was kept by the society — or its officers — with any individual member. This at first always surprises the thoughtful visitor and appears to be a gross laxity of business procedure, but there was no need of "bookkeeping;" there could be no charge against, or credit to a member and hence no balance to be struck. What was the property of one was the property of all. The trustees allotted the proper portion to each individual or family. Each person was permitted two suits of clothes a year. The material would be submitted in a limited variety and quality; each would select the cloth and the tailors made the men's suits and the seamstresses the women's dresses. Often the women made their own dresses and knit their own stockings and those for the men. In former years the attire of the Zoarites was nearly uniform, being very simple and eccentric in style, somewhat after the fashion of the Quakers. But now-a-days their apparel is much the same as one might see in any American village. They are neat in appearance and their clothes are kept in better order and repair than is usually the case. The women wore the homely sun bonnet. Luxuries, such as jewelry and ornamental articles of dress were, of course, unsupplied and unworn. Each man was however entitled to a plain, silver watch and watch and clock repairing was one of the assigned occupations.

Until recent years the material for their clothing was almost entirely made by the Society. They raised their own flax and wool and in their mills wove both woolen and linen cloths; this was done to the extent of selling these goods in large quantities to outsiders. These factories were both closed at the date of my visit. For some time they had ceased to export their fabrics, but on the contrary had purchased the material, at least in part, for their own clothing. The Society could buy cloth cheaper than it could make it. Indeed this was true of nearly all their industries which formerly were numerous and flourishing and not only produced all necessary commodities for their comfortable existence, but also afforded large and profitable commerce with the outside world. Their location upon the Tuscarawas river gave them a valuable and unfailing water power and they had two large flour mills, a saw mill, planing mill, machine shop, tannery, dye house, stove foundry, cooper shop, woolen mill, brewery, slaughter house, blacksmith shop, tile works, pottery, etc. In all these concerns when in successful operation the best of goods were produced both as to quality of material and honesty of manufacture, and their goods were eagerly sought by foreign customers. But during the present generation these enterprises have declined and ceased to be profitable — the age of invention and improvement in machinery, the multiplicity of outside manufactures and the fierce contest of competition had undermined and crushed many of their manufacturing interests. The Zoarites are not a progressive people; they do not keep pace in their business methods with the times— the changes in appliance and the modes of conducting commercial affairs became too rapid for their adoption, and from being producers they have become consumers, relying mostly upon the outer world to supply their needs.

Up to a few years ago they obtained the hides from their cattle and made their leather for their shoes; that was long since abandoned, as they could buy leather for less than the cost of making; and their chief shoemaker informed them that they were foolish to continue making their shoes, as they could obtain them ready made better and cheaper. But he added, "We have not the money to buy all them things, so we keep on making our clothes and shoes." Formerly it was the rule that the members get an order from the trustees on the shoemaker for their shoes. Latterly this has not been required. One needing "foot gear" simply resorted to the shoe shop, had his measure taken and patiently bided the time of the leisurely cobbler. For many years in the past the Zoar shoe shop did a thriving business with the outside countrymen. But now the shrewd farmers buy the machine made article, elsewhere, for less money.

The stove foundry long ago closed up—the stoves cast were grotesquely large and cumbersome. When the sale for the original pattern ceased they attempted to make no others. The stoves outside might grow light and graceful and economical in the consumption of fuel, but the Zoar heaters remained large, heavy and homely as ever.

The machine shop, planing and saw mill were all in operation, as was the larger flouring mill, the latter under the management of Peter Bimeler, a direct descendant in the third generation from the noted Joseph. This mill is most picturesquely located just south of the village on the main road from Canal Dover. It is not far from the river and the mill race runs through a cluster of noble and venerable forest trees, while across the roadway and upon the slope of the hill are the home and grounds of the miller, just named. His house is famous for containing a pipe organ, made entirely by Mr. Peter Bimeler. The wind department of the instrument is ingeniously run by a cable extending to the mill and propelled by the same power that drives the grist wheels. Mr. Bimeler is not only a genius in invention and mechanical construction, but also he is one in music. Without ever having had any instruction from professional or amateur teachers, he plays readily and most skillfully the most classical and the most popular music. It has been remarked that music seems to be the only direction in which the Zoarites display any talent, but that, it may be said, is common to the German people. There were, however, no educated musicians in Zoar. Worldly music was prohibited by the more fervid in religion. They used a hymn book, but sang sparingly in their church services. They had for some time maintained an orchestra, which, I was told, did most creditable work. It was led by Mr. Louis Zimmerman, the energetic secretary of the Society, and an accomplished musician. Mr. Zimmerman seemed to be the promoter and leader of whatever social life Zoar could boast. The Zoar brass band was an institution of some years' standing. I did not see a piano nor an organ in any of the houses, save that described above and the one in their church. I was much entertained one morning by watching a band of four or five Italian musicians, tambourine and banjo girls, led by the inevitable organ grinder, as they strolled and played through the village. The children flocked to hear the music, much as children do anywhere, but there were no demonstrations of joy or glee, and greatly to the disgust of the players, who evidently did not understand the peculiar character of their audience; there were no pennies thrown; "not one cent for tribute"—it was not a cash community—strange anomaly, money did not circulate in that civilization. Music, nevertheless, timid and primitive as it seemed to be, constituted apparently the only form of recreation in which Zoar ever indulged.

The hum-drum of Zoar life was relieved during the summer months by the visitors who frequented the place. Zoar is a favorite destination for excursion parties and these are accommodated in a large and attractive grove called the Park, just west of the village and overlooking the valley and river of Tuscarawas. This custom of permitting and even encouraging visitors is an innovation of late years and one not calculated to advance the welfare of the community, which is thus brought in contact with the outside life and a phase of it not always the most desirable. The Zoar people in their life were almost devoid of amusements. Their religion prohibited dancing; they had no social nor literary nor even musical entertainments. Such a thing as a lecture or concert or public entertainment of any kind seemed to be, nay was, entirely foreign to Zoar. Nor so far as I could learn had they any diversions in the home circle. Nor did they seem to miss the pastimes of modern society. Perhaps their life, free from care, worry and hurry, and excessive physical labor and mental exertion required little or no relaxation. Their temperament, moreover, was sedate· and stolid. They showed less sense of humor than the German generally manifests. Though on the other hand they were uniformly affable and good natured, perhaps more so than the average German. Occasionally a gleam of facetiousness would break through their earnest conversation. One would imagine that their isolated and fraternal form of life would intensify sociability; probably it did; they knew each other as one family and owing to their close and continued contact many families were intermarried. Marital relationship and proximity of residence is not always promotive of friendliness, but the Zoarites constituted to an exceptional degree a happy family.

My first visit was made in the summer of 1898, after their determination to divide the property and dissolve the Society, but some months before either of those purposes were accomplished. Preparations were in process for the distribution, such as the surveying and appraising of the land. The old regime of the society was still in full force, but they were inclined just then to be some somewhat suspicious of visitors from fear of interference with their affairs or the acquiring by outsiders of information which they did not wish imparted to the public. It was in the afternoon that I arrived at the Zoar hotel, an overwhelmingly large hostelry for so small a town. The old hotel, erected half a century ago, stands on the main street, and extending east on the corner for fully a hundred and fifty feet, has had added to its front a modern structure three stories in height and containing some fifty commodious rooms. A wide veranda surrounds the new addition on the west front and south side. This new wing was added some five or six years since to accommodate the large number of summer boarders who frequent Zoar to spend a longer or shorter time enjoying the beautiful scenery, the rural drives of the surrounding country and the quaint and quiet life of the village. The old landlord greeted me respectfully, but hardly with that personal zeal and financial interest usually displayed by the professional hosts in their new guests. From majority he had been allotted to "run the hotel." He was moreover a trustee of the society and a man of unusual general intelligence and special knowledge of the affairs of the Zoarites. The hotel corps, cooks, waiters, etc., were assigned to their duties as their respective portions in the labor of the Society. The cuisine was countrified but creditable—not quite the usual hotel variety, but all wholesome, well cooked and all the articles of diet were the "real thing," as they were genuine home productions and could be trusted without the test of the state "pure food" inspection. There was a "bar"—the only one in Zoar—in the corner room of the hotel, where beer and wines were served; the latter mostly of the village vintage. The beer drank in this region had heretofore been solely that of Zoar brewing, noted for its purity and excellency. The brewery had recently shut down and an importation was now all that could be had. It could be bought cheaper than made. The Zoarites drank beer freely. This beverage, fresh from the brewery, when in operation, was supplied to each family in generous quantities each day, precisely as was milk and cider. But they were a sober people; rarely did a case of intoxication occur. The income to the hotel from whatever source, bar, board or livery, went, of course, to the society fund, as did all revenues received from any source; none went to the landlord or any of the hotel force.

Across the street, opposite the hotel, was the only store of the place; a general country store, where dry goods, groceries, hardware, etc., were provided for the outside country customers, the neighboring farmers. This merchandizing establishment was conducted in the interests of the Society and did a large and profitable business. Mr. Louis Zimmermann, the secretary and treasurer of the Society, was the manager of this, as he was of all the negotiations between the Society and outside parties. In this store room was the postoffice of the village. This store and the hotel opposite formed the center of the village life and here the male members who were so inclined spent their lounging hours, smoking, chatting and discussing the affairs of their community. Their conversation was mostly in German, not a very pure form, but rather a peasant dialect. Nearly all could speak English. They were not an educated people, though all adults could read and write in German. They were not a reading class. Literature of any description was conspicuously absent in this community. There was no library in the place; books were a rarity in the homes. Some of the Zoarites were subscribers to a weekly (generally German) paper, but that was an exception. In former years the admission of outside literature was discouraged, if not forbidden as tending to weaken their religious faith and make inroads into the principles and practices of their life. On the contrary, they never attempted to propagate their doctrines among outsiders. They never sought converts. No paper or periodical of any kind was ever printed or published by the Society. They took little or no interest in the concerns of the outside world, unless it was in national politics. This lack of interest was true of the older people but did not apply so much to the younger generation. They were all loyal American citizens. In the Rebellion, in spite of their peace principles, many enlisted and fought for the preservation of the Union, and the

Society had its quota of veterans. None, I was told, took part in the late Spanish war. They took an interest in national events, particularly in the campaign of 1896, when as the election returns showed, almost to a man they voted the Republican ticket. The money issue of that campaign must have seemed rather extraneous to their personal inter-dealings. The question may have had a bearing on the commercial relations of the Society with outsiders, but among themselves they had no need of nor use for money. Everything they permitted themselves to have or enjoy was provided to the individual "without money and without price." In this respect they, the older ones especially, were to be regarded as in the position of wards of an estate. I wondered what they would do when given their property and placed upon their own responsibility, exertion and resources. There were, in a partisan sense, no local politics in Zoar, though there was not an absence of municipal functions. Once a year the members of the society met in the Town Hall, situated in a small frame building erected for that purpose, and in the little belfry of which hung the bell that called the people to work in the morning and sounded the dinner and quitting hour. In this little hall the members would gather, hear reports from their officers, consider their questions, discuss their interests and hold their elections.

In 1884 (August 25) when the railroad came along and established a station at Zoar and put the village in steam touch with the world, the Zoarites incorporated[22] their village and assumed municipal form, with a mayor, town council, marshal, etc. But in the election of these officials there was never any division of any kind. No partisan contests disturbed the even tenor of Zoar life. Their elections were monotonous and unanimous. The municipal officers were chosen from the leading members of the Society and at the time of my visit Jacob Sturm, one of the three trustees, was the Mayor as well. He was also the railway station agent. His earnings belonged to the Society.

As the evening shades began to fall an interesting scene was presented by "the lowing herd winding slowly" from the

---

[22] These Articles of Incorporation will be found in latter part of this article.

pasture to the village barn. There were "ninety and nine" of them, many with their clanging bells, driven, or rather accompanied, by one of the Zoarite patriarchs, who bore on his bent shoulders the burden of more than three-score and ten years. The sleek kine filed leisurely down the lane into either side of the basement of an immense barn. The name of each cow was posted in large letters over her stall and each found without hesitation her own proper place. A dozen or more Zoar lasses, with pails and stools, cheerily entered upon the task of milking, superintended by the stable "boss." The cattle and barn were clean and tidy and this milking scene was a memorable one, The milk was carried into a small dairy close by, placed in large cans, and here dealt out to the village housewives or children who came with their buckets to receive their portion. The barn was a lofty concern, and in the upper story was kept hay and feed for the cattle. There were two other extensive buildings or sets of buildings used in connection with the farming department. On the eastern edge of the village were the stables where were kept all the horses, some fifty or more in number, and in adjoining buildings the wagons, farm implements, machines, etc. The horses were well fed and cared for, though this stable establishment had a decidedly neglected and dilapidated appearance.

On a hill still to the east of the village was an enormous "L" shaped sheep shed with the red tile roof, which, owing to the elevation on which the buildings stood, could be seen from almost any direction for a long distance. At one time wool raising was a very great feature in their industrial life, but the flock of sheep now only numbered two or three hundred. In the good old times it had often numbered more than a thousand. Not far from the horse stable was the cider mill, which was in full blast, producing an article of superior quality. When in season this was daily carted about the village in a low-wheeled, large-barrelled conveyance, precisely resembling a small sprinkling wagon. It stopped at every door and the inmates were supplied with a pail full or more, as was required.

Not far from the hotel was the laundry where the washing was done for the community. Near by was a stunted, one-story, sullen, ominous, looking structure with small, iron-grated windows and a heavy double plank door. It was the Zoar Bastille; they called it the "calaboose." I inquired with much surprise as to the necessity for this penal institution in so moral and sober a community, and was informed with a smile on the part of my respondent, that it was built solely for the benefit of visitors to the village. It came with the incorporation of the town and the town marshal. Zoar was, as before stated, a favorite field for the pleasure seeker and occasionally the excursionist exhiliration reached a boisterous and even belligerent stage, and incarceration was the only remedy. In the days when the tramp was so numerously abroad in the land, Zoar was his haven and delight, as the generous and sympathetic Zoarite would "take him in," feed him and lodge him over night in the lockup. But my informant proudly stated the Zoarites themselves never had any use for a prison. No community of like number and age ever had such a record for morality and good behavior. From the origin of the Society no Zoarite, while a member of the Society, was ever charged with a felony or crime. These remarkable statements were verified by several of the oldest inhabitants; certainly the highest testimony to the perfect character and spotless life of the Separatists. It is doubtful whether any community in any time or place can produce such a record.

At the northern outskirts of the village upon rising ground that overlooked the whole settlement were the bakery, church and schoolhouse. The bakery was an interesting relic of the old time, primeval bake ovens. The family having in charge this important feature of the Society's provision department, were assigned a good sized corner dwelling, with a roomy, stone floored kitchen into the rear of which was built a cavernous brick oven, the cooking chamber of which was elevated about two feet from the level of the kitchen floor. This oven was large enough for a man to easily enter and crawl about when repairs were necessary. The heating apartment was a similar brick chamber, not under but at the side of the bake oven. Here most of the baking was done for the village, though all of the families cooked more or less for themselves. The schoolhouse and church were brick buildings

of many years standing.   The schoolhouse was a two story structure with a spacious recitation room on each floor.   This property
was dedicated by the Society to the Township school authorities.
The school was conducted in all respects like any village school,
under the state school laws.   The township school trustees elected
the teacher and paid him from the public school fund.   For fifteen or sixteen years the only teacher has been Mr. Levi Bimeler,
a great-grandson of Joseph Bimeler.   He obligingly showed me
through the school building and I found him a gentleman of ability
and culture.   He had been fitted for his profession by attending
the public schools at Strasburg (Tuscarawas county) and the
Normal Schools at Shanesville and New Philadelphia.   These
outside educational advantages, improved by Mr. Bimeler, were
at the expense of the Society and so far as I could learn this
was the only instance in which a member had been sent away
or been permitted to leave temporarily for the purpose of being
educated.

He held his certificate from the county board as any public
school teacher.   He was paid the salary of fifty dollars per month,
which of course under the rules of the community he turned into
the treasury of the Society.   It was vacation when I visited the
building and I did not see the school in operation.   Mr. Bimeler
informed me that there were ninety-five pupils enrolled and about
sixty-five in average attendance.   This number embraced, however, many children not belonging to the Zoar society or village,
but residing in this school territory, children of outside neighboring farmers.

Might not this collateral education of the Zoar young and
the "worldly" youth have been a dangerous influence upon the
growth or retention of the principles of the Zoarites in their boys
and girls?

All the Zoarite children attended school from the ages of six
to fifteen with the girls, and to sixteen in case of the boys.   The
pupils, their tutor testified were bright, attentive, studious and
obedient.   The course covered the main studies of the primary and
grammar grades.   There were a few studies that might be classed
as in the high school curriculum.   The instruction was in English except on two days in the week, when they were taught Ger-

man. Music was a favorite study and in that the pupils did well. The children of the village with whom I talked seemed intelligent, well behaved and obedient, and less forward and "pert" in manner than the average American youth of similar age.

The village church if not orthodox in its faith was so in its furniture with its old fashioned, straight back seats. The walls and ceilings were uncolored and unadorned; the whole air of the interior was cold and uninviting. A melodeon was on the platform near the desk. On the open space back of the seats stood one of the colossal Zoar stoves, with a capacity sufficient to absorb the contents of a small coal mine at one divine service. But coal in those parts was plenty as the lands of the Society were well supplied with this mineral, though it was not of the best grade. Before the decline of interest in religious observances, the services were three on the Sabbath; a Sunday school in the afternoon and worship exercises in the morning and evening. There were no prayers — only a song or two and the reading of one of Bimeler's discourses. This reading had lately been done by the village gardener who acted as both florist and parson. Bimeler's homilies had been read and re-read till they had become an old story and interest in them was sadly waning. Much that they contained had become obsolete in the Zoar belief. Attendance upon church was not obligatory and the audiences were slowly dwindling in number and zeal. All services had been abandoned at the time of my visit, and as one member remarked, their religious sentiment was passing away, as a prelude to the departure of their communism. The descendants of the pioneer and pious Separatists clung no longer to the plain and simple faith of their fathers. But while there seemed to be an abatement of religious life in the Society there was no lessening in the standard of their moral conduct. The church was not used for the ceremonies usually celebrated in the sanctuary. The funerals and weddings did not take place in the kirk. There was no religious observance in marriage. It was purely a civil contract, the legal part being performed by a justice of the peace. In 1898, and for some years previous, the secretary of the Society held the office of justice of the peace, and discharged all the duties of the same. They did not permit members to marry outside of the society, and required all who made outside matrimonial alliances to leave the community. When marriage first began among them the plan was adopted that the children should remain in the care of their parents until three years of age, when they were housed in a common children's home, the girls in one and the boys in another, where each respectively were brought up under the direction of persons appointed for that purpose; nor did they ever again come under the exclusive control of their parents. This custom prevailed until 1845, when it was discontinued and thereafter the children were reared in the homes of and by their parents, subject to the jurisdiction of the trustees, to the extent that their authority invaded the domestic life. It was the business of the Society, through the trustees, to provide for the children all they required, until they became of age and elected to become members of the Society.

The funerals were very simple affairs, there being no ceremony of any kind either at the house or at the burial. The encased body, in an open wagon, followed by the villagers on foot, was quietly conveyed to the grave at the usual hour of 1 P. M. The following Sunday evening a funeral sermon was read in the church. The cemetery, situated on a hill northwest of the village, was a veritable "God's acre;" densely shaded by fir trees, the grounds almost without paths and profusely overgrown with grass, wild flowers, creeping vines and weeds. Until a few years ago, tombstones were proscribed. The graves were not even designated. Bimeler requested that no monument mark his sepulchre, and none does. I could not find it, though its location is well known to his people. It is now the custom to have the graves marked by a wooden head-piece or in some cases by a stone slab.

Such were the more noticeable external features, as presented to me during my few days' sojourn in Zoar. They were a unique and in many respects remarkable people, leading a peculiar and isolated life. Their daily needs and simple wants were all readily supplied. Their lives were peaceful and easeful, proof of the sad refrain of Anna Boleyn:

> " 'Tis better to be lowly born,
> And range with humble livers content."

The men looked well fed and ruddy and moved about with a deliberation at times almost amounting to indifference. The women were noticeably the busier and more active. In the earlier period of the community they shared almost equally the physical labors of the men. They cleared the forest and tilled the field no less than their husbands and sons. After the Society reached its prosperous stage, the lot of the women was an easier one. Their household cares were lighter than is usually the case with housewives. But they did not appear as hale and hearty as the men, perhaps, possibly, because they confined themselves indoors more than is generally the habit with the village dame. But they were happy and contented. Their domestic life was serene and pleasant. This is evidenced by the astounding fact that there had never been a divorce in the Society. At the time of my visit the wives, though consenting to the coming change in the community, were more anxious than their husbands as to the outcome.

To one from the hurly-burly of the business world the village of Zoar seemed oppressed with an air of stillness, if not even sluggishness. Hamlet could have walked the streets of Zoar for a stage and have truly remarked:

> "And enterprises of great pith and moment,
> With this regard their currents turn away,
> And lose the name of action."

What did the Zoarites themselves think of it? Did they regard it as a success? Did they wish to change this life to one of individual responsibility and result?

The patriarch, whose duty it was to drive the cows to pasture at early morn and to the barn at dewy eve, did not wish to give up the Zoarite scheme. Communism with him had been and still was a success. This was the sentiment of many of the older members— it was too late for them to launch out into the world on an untried experience for themselves; many of them succumbed reluctantly and apprehensively to the will of the great majority — in the decision to disband. To them it was a life free from care, worry and excessive work. They literally took no thought for the morrow. They lay down in comfortable homes at night, in certain and satisfactory knowledge that they would be equally well provided for, on the succeeding day.   What boon in life greater or more desirable than that?

> "From toil, his spirits light,
> From busy day the peaceful night,
> Rich, from the very want of wealth
> In heaven's best treasures, peace and health."

The Zoar region was a remarkably healthy one; the pure and wholesome food, their simple and regular habits, all united to prevent disease and prolong life.

There was one doctor in the Society, the only one they had known for a generation.   His office was a room or two in one of the less attractive buildings near the hotel.   He was self-educated; had "picked up" his medical knowledge; his nostrums were few and simple and nature was doubtless his chief assistant; his "school", if he had any, might be called "the school of common sense."   In extremely difficult cases an outside surgeon might be called in.

"Yes," said the doctor in his chat with me, "the old ones are not so anxious to quit but the young ones are bound to wind up. They go out and get a taste of the world and its opportunities and activities and they become discontented and restless."

And that was true; many a family had a son in the great west or some large city.   The young men wanted to start out for themselves and possess and control the results of their efforts.   The barber shop was a little back room allotted for that purpose in the town hall building.   Two days in the week the members, who were addicted to the custom, were shaven and also such visitors as were in need of tonsorial attention.   The knight of the razor was a bright young fellow who gave me fair facial treatment, and with the customary barber's conversational powers imparted much information as I plied him with questions.   He was of age, born and raised in the Society but did not care to become a member.   "No chance here for a young man."   He contemplated going off to "find a job" elsewhere; wanted to do for himself; had already "worked several years and had nothing to show for it."   But as he was eligible to probation and membership he hoped by remaining with the community until the distribution that he might get half a share. There were several in the same situation.   As I gave him the price

MAIN STREET LOOKING NORTH.

of his labor (shave) he remarked if he were his own man he would get that, while now "it goes to the Society." He thought it was better for all that they divide up.

The blacksmith, a stalwart six footer, testified he had worked hard all his life with an indefinite undivided property interest as his reward. "Think how much I would have now had I worked and saved for myself — some in the Society have done hardly any work, but will get the same that I do. This way of doing business is not natural, nor right," he added.

I found several who touched on this note — that those put at the hard or difficult, or continuous tasks felt that others were not so heavily burdened — yet the recompense was precisely the same. One whose task began at times at daylight and did not end till night was very "sore" at some who got off with "easy jobs." This feeling of the inequality of the exertion put forth and of the labor performed was very often expressed in no undisguised terms. Yet all admitted it was not the fault of the authorities in their efforts to assign and equalize the work. The trustees tried to be fair and judicious in the apportionment. It was natural for some to work. It was equally natural in some to shirk. Said one of the most intelligent and observant in the Society: "This system of communism puts a premium on indolence." It deadened the spurs and motives of activity. Some one has said man is naturally a lazy animal, he only works because he has to. Human nature is prone to seek the paths that present the least resistance. Communism affords favorable conditions for the discouragement of energy and the exercise of the inertia.

I was not a little amused at my encounter with the "boss" of the barn. He was silently engaged in extracting the lacteal wealth from one of the patient kine — that prosaic process commonly called milking. I approached and addressed him in English, eliciting no response. I then tried my German, rusty from disuse and many years absence from its Fatherland. He evidently preferred my better American to my bad German. To my queries he acknowledged he heartily favored a distribution and a chance for himself. The communistic system gave the lazy too much leeway. He toiled while others slept. Finally to spike my battery of inter-

4

rogatories he asked, "Was you one of dem newspaper fellers what wants to know evertings?" "No," I replied, "I am a college professor." "Oh, vell," he instantly retorted, "dot was the same ting and just as bad." We understood each other perfectly after that and became good friends.

In the hot boiler room of the cider mill I found one of the oldest members who seemed to be the personification of contentment. He was, and for many years had been, the fireman and he sat in his bared arms eating an apple and apparently wrapt in pleasing meditation. I think he must have been thinking of the approaching dismemberment of the community, for upon my asking his views he unhesitatingly stated he had keenly enjoyed the Zoar life. It had been one of plenty and peace. But he realized there had come a changed condition of affairs and he philosophically accepted the "new dispensation." "Yes," he said, "I was satisfied and happy. It was all right till a few years yet. I know not how it will do in the new way, but we must make the change, dat was sure."

The good old shoemaker who, with two younger assistants, was "pegging away" in a faithful but deliberate manner, was in favor of the dissolution, though a little uncertain and uneasy about the outcome to himself and some others. All three agreed it was "not according to nature for one to work for others," "it is better that each be by himself and know what he has got." The element of self-interest and individuality was self-assertive. The principle, "every man for himself," was a popular sentiment. Many minor influences had been working to undermine the Society. Opportunities had been increasing as time passed for the shrewd and enterprising ones to acquire sums of money in a way that did not demand, in their estimation, its being turned into the general fund. This developed in some curious and ingenious ways. Many families raised chickens in their yards; these and the eggs they would sell to outsiders. This questionable method of traffic created much dissatisfaction and the trustees endeavored at times to regulate and equalize the poultry production — by dictating the number of fowls each family might raise. This attempt was found difficult to enforce. Housewives would take in washing for the visitors; the young and older too would do sewing for the summer boarders, or make lace and various articles for sale; the boys would catch and sell fish; make and let boats on the river; slip off after work and do odd jobs for outside parties. Individual effort for personal gain could not be suppressed nor equalized. I was talking with one of the elder members as he sat on his porch when a young man rode up on a Columbia wheel, dismounted and entered the house. He was the son of my old friend. I asked if the Society furnished bicycles to the members. The old gentleman laughed and said "not much", and he explained that the young fellow earned money nights working for the railroad and bought a wheel. It was the only safety I saw in Zoar, but the manner of its acquisition was illustrative of one of the currents that was in opposition to the simple communism with which they started. Another source of inequality and dissatisfaction was the furnishing certain members at times with money to go upon trips to see friends or transact some necessary business at a distant point. Those who had no occasion for going objected to or at least regarded with disfavor those who went. Again, and one of the most important items tending toward disruption was the necessity for the Society to employ help. Their principal business had always been farming and stock-raising. This required the continuous labor of many "farm hands." Their farming interest was about the only one left them. The young and stout men were drifting away. The older members were unable to do hard and incessant manual work. There were thousands of acres to care for or go to waste. The Society was driven to the employment of imported help. A field near the cemetery was being plowed by four teams, driven by as many plowmen. I accosted them as Zoarites, only to learn all were "hired help" and foreign to the Society. Some fifty men were on the pay roll of the Society at the time of my visit, all of course non-members. There were also several adult members [by birth] of Zoar families who declined to become members of the Society, but who were permitted to remain in the community and who, in addition to getting their living from the Society, were paid small annual sums for their work. They were of course eligible to membership but for various reasons did not wish to legally join. A main factor in the failure of the Society was the general decline of its industries and the shrinkage in values. To the decline in the industries of the Society I have already referred. The shrinkage in values of both real and personal property was necessarily not confined at this time to the Society. It was common to the country wherever property of any description was to be found.

A few Zoarites acknowledged that the communistic plan fostered extravagance or at least lack of thrift and economy on the part of the members. There was great and unnecessary waste of material, particularly in the line of food and fuel and household necessities. The baker would get from the miller more flour than was actually needed. The consumers drew from the baker more than their needs demanded. Not being required to save for themselves, they naturally did not attempt to save for others or for all. What came so easily and so plentifully was not properly valued and there was no incentive to household economy.

DECISION TO DISBAND.

The history of Zoar is the record of the rise and decline of a communistic civilization. In the pioneer years, their religious zeal and physical necessities impelled them to industry and thrift. After the forming of the communistic contract they prospered as a Society. The country was opening up; the western tide of emigration, as it swept by or settled about them, fostered their industries and enhanced the value of their property. The building of the Ohio Canal was of great benefit to them. They contracted to dig the canal throughout the extent of their territory, by which they not only acquired the sum of $21,000.00 in ready money, but also made a considerable sum by furnishing the neighboring contractors with articles of food.[23]

It was a period of development; of clearing and improving the land; of labor and of saving. They added to their original purchase until at one time they possessed some twelve thousand acres. They not only built up industries for their own consumption, but established a large commerce with the outside

---

[23] Penny Magazine (1837) Vol. VI, page 411.

world. The growth and prosperity of the Society was largely due to the ability and shrewdness of Joseph Bimeler. Until his death the affairs of the community progressed. This success continued, or rather remained undiminished for several years after his death.[24] Then the decline set in and for the past twenty-five years the interests of the Society, as one member put it, "have been going down." Their trade gradually fell off, their income decreased and their expenses increased. Their young and active members deserted. At various times in its history individual members withdrew and made claim for their distributive shares of the accumulated property. More rarely a dissolution was suggested, but such proposal met with little or no encouragement among the members. In the few bygone years the more intelligent and observant among them could not fail to realize that the Society was "auf die Neige" — on the wane —and time alone would determine its dismemberment.

One of the most interesting episodes in the later history of the Society was the outspoken "rebellion" of one of its leading members, Mr. Levi Bimeler, the descendant of Joseph Bimeler and the village school master, of whom we have already made mention.

Mr. Bimeler was educated, as has been noted, outside of the Society. He openly advocated the right of the members to withdraw and receive their distributive share if they desired it. In 1895 Mr. Bimeler promulgated his views in a little folio,—a four-page sheet about the size of a legal cap page. Mr. Bimeler was editor, publisher and pressman. He wrote the entire contents of his paper—a monthly—and then duplicated it upon a letter copying press. The edition was of course very limited, a hundred or more, and sold to the members. It was the only periodical publication ever attempted in Zoar.

---

[24] As late as 1875 their property was estimated at the nominal value of $1,500,000. About the date of Bimeler's death, the society numbered some 500 adults and children. This number in 1885 was 390 according to the statement in Prof. Ely's "Labor Movement in America."

This organ of the agitator was called the "Nugitna" and three numbers were issued, the fourth partially prepared for duplication and publication, when the editor was "called down" by the Society authorities and given to understand that unless he ceased his vexatious and rebellious publication he would be expelled and deprived of all rights, present or prospective, in the Society. The fourth number never appeared. As these monthlies represent an element — however small it may have been — in the Society at the time of their appearance, and as they contribute much information concerning the history and purpose of the Society, they are herewith reproduced without alteration. They have historic interest and deserve permanent preservation in the archives of Zoar.

We would not say that they are to be taken as voicing the popular sentiment at the period of their publication. As the editor frankly confesses, his propaganda met with both approval and disapproval. The exercise of the censorship of the press in this case would indicate a centralized power in this equal community. The "Nugitna", as the reader will observe, was a bugle-blast for individual rights in no mild or mistaken tones. It is the irony of fate that a Bimeler should have been the most pronounced iconoclast of his great-grandfather's institution. The claim for which the "Nugitna" contended was not a new or novel one. It had often been made at various times and by various members who wished to withdraw from the Society and take their "belongings" with them, or by members who had withdrawn. We have already reported the law cases growing out of such claims. But we let the "Nugitna" speak for itself.

THE NUGITNA.

Vol. 1.   Zoar, Ohio, Dec. 30, 1895.   No. 1.

INDEPENDENCE, NOW AND FOREVER!

When, in the course of human events, it becomes necessary for one person to dissolve the political bands which connect him with a Communistic Society, and to assume among the citizens of a state the equal and separate station to which the laws of nature and of nature's God entitle him, a decent respect to the opinions of his fellow Communists requires that he should declare the cause which impel him to such separation. Whenever any form of government becomes destructive of the ends for which it was instituted, it is the right of the governed to amend or abolish it.

Fellow Communists. I quote the above, with slight alterations, from the "Declaration of Independence." It fits our conditions exactly. And, if we possess only half the "grit" and determination of our ancestors, we will be successful in obtaining the coveted liberty and Independence. This Society has for a long time back become destructive of the ends for which it was instituted.

You know—or perhaps you don't—that this "Communistic Society" was instituted for these five ends; viz: 1st. To secure that satisfaction, proceeding from the faithful execution of those principles and duties which the Christian religion demands; 2nd.

To plant and establish the Spirit of Love as the bond of peace and unity; 3rd. To unite our various individual interests into one common stock; 4th. To abolish all distinctions of rank and of fortune; 5th. To live as brethren and sisters of one common family.

We believe that the faithful execution of those "Christian duties" was an easy matter to our forefathers, but that it is not possible for us to do likewise as Communists. We may form the best resolves, and aim to live according to the rules laid down by the founders of this Community, but all of these vanish like a light morning mist, when we see the total corruptness of our whole system. Some, indeed, still believe that this is the system, and can not understand why some have the audacity to condemn it, and to attempt to withdraw therefrom with a proper share of the Society's property. But some day they will have a revelation. Look about you, and show me the man or woman who has secured the desired satisfaction as indicated in the 1st end. There is not one who can truly say it. Examine yourselves, go down into the depths of your conscience and ask yourself — Am I living up to this purpose? — and the answer will surely be negative. To those who say that *they* have lived and are now living in accordance with the 1st end, I can only say that they are the worst hypocrites existing, and that none but their like believe them.

THE NUGITNA

Is published every four weeks. Its aim is to secure to the members of

THE ZOAR SOCIETY

the right to withdraw therefrom, and to receive a proper share of the Society's property.

TERMS:

Local subscribers, per copy, 5 cents; per year 50 cents. By mail, per copy 10 cents; per year, $1.00.

LEVI BIMELER,

Editor and Publisher, Zoar, Ohio.

COMMENTS ON THE MEETING OF DECEMBER 3rd, 1895.

The meeting was opened by Mr. Zimmerman who, in a few, well chosen words, briefly stated the object for which the meeting was called. Mr. Beuter, sr., opened the discussion in his usual way on such occasions — exhorting the members to continue in this state of Communism, but advised also to discard certain avoidable habits of intemperance and gluttony. He was followed by Christ. Ruof jr. who spoke in direct opposition of Mr. Beuter's 1st theme. Next came Jacob Sturm who entertained the meeting by an explanation. Next spoke L. Bimeler who advocated the peaceable dissolution of the bands which connect individual members with the Society. He was ably seconded by Messrs. Sylvan, Kuemmerle and P. J. Bimeler. Charles Ehlers ably presented the real object of the meeting.

Others followed; some acting in a gentlemanly manner as did those who spoke before them, while others lost all control over their tempers and gave vent to their personal feelings against one another.

Christian Ruof sr. was conspicuous through his absence.

The meeting, after completing its object, adjourned wiser than when it met.

A few more such meetings with the people who have no other way of obtaining Data, will work wonders.

TOWN TOPICS.

The time for the annual slaughtering of hogs is at hand. The party of slaughterers began their work on the 16th inst. and disposed of the 1st lot of hogs, 45 head, in less than one week.

John Gantenbein, the barber, was waiter at the butcher's meals. John is a good waiter and always gives satisfaction. On this occasion however, he caught cold—the weather being wet and cool—and was sick for a week after. John says "Das kann mir gestohlen werden"; and "The next time I'll tend to my business only."

The Society is actively engaged in lumbering and is shipping the lumber to all parts of the globe.

Frank Kappel and Rosa Ruof —both born in Zoar but for a number of years away from home—are visiting at their parents. Both look well and happy.

GUESTS AT THE HOTEL.

Mr. Lockwood; Miss Scoti; and A. Gunn.

The "Gold Mine" is flooded.

The entertainment given by the pupils of the Zoar Schools assisted by the classes of '94 and '95 was well attended and gave universal satisfaction. The classes of '94 and '95—all girls between 15 and 18 years of age—made an immense impression on the young men in the audience. Such expressions as "They look like a garden of Roses in bloom"; "Ah, me! I wish she were mine"; "The sweet angels;" and half suppressed sighs were heard on all sides.

COUNCIL PROCEEDINGS.

Dec. 9th. Council met in regular session. No business being on hand Council adjourned.

Mr. and Mrs. Obed Burkhart were made happy. It is a boy.

Mr. Leo. Kern, a veteran of the Civil war, was held up by four armed men on the canal road between Zoar and Zoar Station and robbed of all his money. Poor Leo! He must have felt as bad as when his corps was routed at Chancellorsville by the Rebels.

Barbara Angele, a domestic in the family of Adam Kuemmerle, died Dec. 26th, 1895.

THE NUGITNA.

Vol. I.   *Zoar, Ohio, January 27, 1896.*   *No. 2.*

COMMUNISM — HUMBUGISM!

The second end for which the Society was established is: "To plant and establish the Spirit of Love as the bond of peace and unity." The second end is closely related to the first and, like it, rests chiefly on religious principles. It is *so* easy to form fundamental principles for *others* to observe; but to live according to them ourselves, is quite different. The pioneers of this settlement had originally no inclination to establish Communism, but simply to find a home where they could, without molestation, live according to their dogma. When the first settlers came in 1817, all was still a wilderness, the first winter was very severe, and they suffered great hardships. Among the settlers were many who were not able to earn a living. Since they left Germany for the purpose of religious freedom, the able-bodied were in honor bound to aid the feeble. After a time the old, infirm, feeble and others who were too lazy to work saw that this could not last forever, and that as soon as the religious scruples exerted less influence, they would be neglected and fare badly. They were the ones who began to agitate the Communistic idea. Said they, "We are one in religious belief, let us be one in rank and fortune." The idea was worked up until those in comfortable circumstances — they were the minority — had no choice but to join or to be considered renegades.

Mr. J. Bimeler, " Old Bimeler " as we call him, opposed the

Communistic movement from the first, and was the last man to give his consent. "Old" Bimeler was the Spiritual head of the Separatists and, having joined the Society, it was mainly through his influence, and the then existing circumstances that the Spirit of Love was kept alive. The Society prospered while he lived. Bimeler saw clearly where Communism would lead to; when we read his sermons we find grave doubts expressed regarding the stability of Communism, and the wisdom of establishing this Society. He was right! Where is the "Spirit of Love" now? Where is the bond of peace and unity? Where are the planters and fosterers of this Spirit? Gone, forever! The "Spirit of Love," as we look at it, is embodied in the "Golden Rule," viz.: "Love thy neighbor as thyself." It appears, however, that the majority interpret it thus: "Love thyself and slander thy neighbor." All the simplicity which the founders held dear has given place to extravagance and pomposity. And "thereby hangs a tale!" The founders were really devout believers, not only in word but in deed also. But we who are believers in form only, who not only not believe but ridicule the most sacred of our ancestors' teachings, can't establish this "Spirit" as Communists. None can deny that we don't believe the religious doctrines of our fathers any more. You may, perhaps, say "O, yes! we believe." But where are your deeds to prove it. Now, if we are renegades, or in other words, fell off from the doctrine of religion, why not sever the political bands which tie us to the Society. Shall we continue to be Communists?

THE NUGITNA

Is published every four weeks. Its aim is to secure to members of

THE ZOAR SOCIETY

the right to withdraw therefrom, and to receive a proper share of the Society's property.

TERMS:

Local subscribers, per copy, 5 cents; per year, 50 cents. By mail, per copy, 10 cents; per year, $1.00.

LEVI BIMELER,
Editor and Publisher, Zoar, Ohio.

COMMENTS.

The appearance of the first number of the "Nugitna" created quite an excitement. Various were the remarks and opinions expressed by different members of the Society. Some were mad, others shook their heads, and still others were glad. The editor has, personally, heard only a few opinions expressed, but is, nevertheless, well informed regarding the prevailing opinions. The first week after the publication of "The Nugitna" there was some strong talk. Some went so far as to express themselves thus: This act is enough to expel the publisher from the Society; but when the cool, second thought came, the impracticability of such expulsion made itself manifest. This "second thought" is a great blessing. "Expel him" is more easily said than done. The U. S. Constitution guarantees freedom of speech and press. We avail ourselves of this guarantee for a good purpose. "The Nugitna" created more stir than anything we can think of in the history of this Society (except perhaps the circulation of a petition in the year 1850–4, for the purpose of throwing the trustees, Ackerman and Sylvan from office and putting the originators of the petition in their place). We can't see why the "Nugitna" should disturb our affairs. We are not seeking to throw anybody from and putting ourselves in the place as those petitioners in the early fifties. No! we simply desire that receding members shall receive a proper share of the Society's property. If we deem it necessary we will publish the petition mentioned above and the names connected with it.

"All is quiet on the Potomac."

THE NUGITNA.

Vol. I.   Zoar, Ohio, February 24, 1896.   No. 3.

COMMUNISM — DESPOTISM.

The 3rd end for which the Society was instituted is "To unite our various individual interests into one common stock." This, like the preceding two rests on Religion, being a modification of the 22nd verse, 18th chapter of St. Luke. Living up to this end required very little self-denial of our forefathers as the majority possessed nothing but what they carried on their backs. The few who were in possession of money had no chance to spend it. The circumstances then and now are widely different. The Pioneers had absolutely no intercourse with the outside world, except a few who were entrusted with the conveyance of goods and produce to, and from Philadelphia, Pa. So you see, that the money one might have did him no particle of good. He could not buy anything if he wanted to. There was equality of fortune among the first settlers. But let us look at the conditions of things as they exist now. Is there a union of individual interests now? Do we contribute every thing into one common stock? Has not the individual interest gained supremacy over the general interest? We tell you that the individual interest is the primary and the general interest the secondary object from the preacher down to the lowliest, with only a *few* exceptions. All this has been brought about by time, intercourse with the outside world, and last, but not least, our Public Schools. The state of affairs now existing is natural and in accordance with the laws of human nature. The present generation sees too clearly that a favored few enjoy all the comforts and luxuries that money can buy, while they must be satisfied with what is meted out to them. This went well thirty years ago, when the members of the Society, were kept in ignorance of the true state of things, when the members did not dare to think contrary to prevailing customs, not to speak of voicing them, for fear of expulsion from the Society. There has always been, and to a certain extent still is a tendency to keep the affairs of the Society from the knowledge of the members. Is it because those in office are the wise men of the Society? Or, are the members too ignorant to be trusted with the knowledge of the Society's affairs. Which?

The secret of the stability of the Society lay in its Children's Institution. In the early history of Zoar, every child when it had attained to the age of three years was taken away from the parents into the Society Children's Institution and left to the tender (?) mercies of its keepers. In some future issue we will illuminate said Institution.

If "Old" Ackerman had done no other good deed but to refuse to send his child to this Institution, he has, by that alone, richly earned the love and esteem of the members which he possessed. Hold sacred the relation of parent to child.

A PIONEER COTTAGE.

THE NUGITNA

Is published every four weeks. Its aim is to secure to members of

THE ZOAR SOCIETY

the right to withdraw therefrom, and to receive a proper share of the Society's property.

TERMS:

Local subscribers, per copy, 5 cents; per year, 50 cents. By mail, per copy, 10 cents; per year, $1.00.

LEVI BIMELER,

Editor and Publisher, Zoar, Ohio.

COMMENTS.

The opposition which " The Nugitna " has encountered continues. The authorities are making strenuous efforts to compel the publisher to quit the business. He said that the " The Nugitna " would not be issued any more if the gross violations of our by-laws, now existing to the full knowledge of the authorities, were also abated.

However, an amicable settlement of the difficulties may yet be reached; in this case " The Nugitna " will be a thing of the past. There are some sections of our by-laws which are unjust, unfair and unconstitutional. " The Nugitna " wants to educate the members of the Society to see that our by-laws need revision. To bring them to look upon Communism as not consistent with modern civilization; and to inculcate a spirit which holds sacred the rights of individual members to obtain and hold private property. The early history of Jamestown, Va., shows that Communism is a failure. Those settlers tried the experiment but gave it up within five years. Is it a wonder then, that we, living in the rich State of Ohio, consider it a failure, too? Communism puts a premium on idleness, and discounts diligence. There is no reward for the industrious, and no punishment for the idle. "Nimms easy und lasz fuenfe grad sein," is appropriate for Communists.

TOWN TOPICS.

We have the sad duty to announce the demise of one of our members. The deceased "Christina Peterman," was the the first child born in Zoar. At the time of her birth the

Zoar Society did not exist yet. She was born July, 1818, in a rough log cabin, and attained to the age of 77 years. Her parents were very wealthy and when Communism was established they gave all into the common fund. In her the Society loses one of its truest members. There is not a soul in Zoar who can say ill of her, but one and all praise her kindness and devotion. The words of Christ may well be applied: "Blessed are the meek: for they shall inherit the earth. Blessed are the pure in heart: for they shall see God. Blessed are the peacemakers: for they shall be called the children of God."

May she rest in peace for evermore.

COUNCIL PROCEEDINGS.

Feb. 10th, 1896. Council met in regular session with all the members present. Minutes of the previous meeting were read and approved. Several subjects were discussed but no action was taken, and on motion of Mr. Beuter, the Council adjourned.

The activity in our lumber industry continues. It is somewhat difficult to haul the lumber owing to the bad condition of the roads.

The Pres. of the Lawrence Tp. school board, Mr. D. Bender, visited our schools. Mr. Bender is well qualified for his office.

The anniversary of the birth of Washington was fittingly celebrated by our schools. The primary room was beautifully decorated with bunting and flags. Both schools met in said room and the exercises were opened with the song "America." Then followed dialogues, speeches, biographies, drills. Many householders were present and joined in the concluding song: Red, White and Blue.

THE NUGITNA.

Vol. 1.   *Zoar, Ohio, March 23, 1896.*   *No. 4.*

COMMUNISM — SOCIALISM.

Communism may be a good thing in the interior of Africa, but in the center of the highly civilized state of Ohio it is an outrage. Communism, as practicably demonstrated by the Zoar Society, abolishes all distinctions of rank and of fortune. Any casual visitor to Zoar will undoubtedly notice the lack of reverence of inferiors to their superiors in age; attainments, or otherwise. This very lack of reverence is a certain means of downfall of all Communistic societies. The smallest child is put on a level with the adult, socially, the toper with the sober, the indolent with the diligent. What other can be expected from such a social order of things, but in the end contentions and ruin. And as to the abolition of fortune distinctions, Phew!— Who has not observed the great difference between high and low of the Zoar Society? Only fools, religious bigots or self-conceited ones are so blind to believe there is no difference in rank and fortune. Tell me, thou Thomas, why the common laborer remains laborer, and the aristocrat remains aristocrat. Is it because all distinction of rank and fortune have been abolished from amongst us? What fools we are to labor on for the benefit of a few favored ones; to keep the Don Juans in their positions of ease, luxury and revelry. The common laborer of any Communistic Society is a mere slave. He must do the work assigned him; eat and drink what is given him; wear what is furnished him and dwell in the house assigned him, all without murmuring; while other members who are more favorably situated, buy for themselves what they want, although the principles of Communism abolish all distinction of rank and of fortune. This statement may easily be verified by a few days sojourn in Zoar. This is Practical Communism. Theorists may dream of a golden time when the Communism shall pervade this whole earth, but let them go to a Communistic Society and fill the place of a common laborer and they will awake to the fact that Purgatory is a blessing compared with their position. Communism is a curse to any and all communities where it is established. It deadens all push, energy and ambition. It puts a premium on idleness and unfits a person for the battle with the world for an existence when the time comes in which he will be thrown on his own resources, which will sooner or later, come to all members of Communistic Societies. There is no equality of rank and fortune in Communistic Societies nor any other intelligent community.

NOTE.—This number (4) of the *Nugitna* was only written as far as here quoted and was never printed nor given to the public.— E. O. R.

DISTRIBUTION OF THE PROPERTY.

The *Nugitna* was premature in its pronounced views. Like all reform organs it had to be radical to receive recognition. Yet the belief was well lodged and growing with many that the communistic feature of the Society had survived its usefulness. The idea of dissolution had become food for thought and topic for discussion. Leading minds and officials among the Zoarites recognized the inevitable approach of the end. Debts were increasing, revenues decreasing and perhaps financial failure was only a question of time. The matter was gradually brought to the notice of the members of the Society, and culminated in a meeting held in early part of January, 1898, when the momentous question was formally broached and the conclusion reached that it was best, if not imperative, that a division of the property be made. One who was present at that meeting related to me its affecting and amusing incidents. It was not without its pathetic scenes. To many it was like the separation after a life journey as one family. The incomprehension of many of the material interests involved in this action, and their inability to appreciate the main issues to be considered, was illustrated in the fact that the chief difficulty to be encountered, in the minds of several, was the equitable disposal of the stoves used in common in many instances by two families who occupied adjoining rooms, and shared one kitchen. Who would get the stove? And how would they separate the kitchen? But these problems were finally temporarily waived or satisfactorily settled and a formal agreement was reached, binding all to the decision to divide the property upon an equitable basis. On March 10th, 1898, the members signed a written compact, whereby the members "selected and appointed Samuel Foltz, Henry S. Fisher and William Becker, commissioners to make said partition and division and to designate in their report and statement by numbers and on a plat to be prepared by George E. Hayward, the Surveyor selected by us, the parts and portions of said real estate which each of us is to receive as our re-

spective shares and allotments."[25]   These Commissioners met
May 2, 1898, and the work of surveying and appraising was
begun May 12th following.   There were at this time two hundred and twenty-two people, adults and children, in the Zoar
Society.   There were one hundred and thirty-six members
entitled to one equal share each, including several (eight or
ten) probationist candidates, who were eligible to membership
by birth, and life in the Society, and it was agreed to pacify
these "could be" members, that they should receive each a
full share.   The appraisement and surveying was in process
at the time of my first visit.   The value of the property of the
Society at this time was of course largely a matter of
conjecture.   The real estate consisted in round numbers of seven
thousand three hundred acres.   This, as I learned by con-
sulting the records of the County Auditor, was placed upon the
tax duplicate at $340,820.00.   The personal property was listed
at $16,250.00.   The division and distribution of the property
was finally accomplished in the fall of 1898.   The Society before
the division, made a contract of sale of the timber upon their
lands.   This sale brought the Society some $15,000.00 in ready
money or short time notes.   There was also a sale of all the
personal property belonging to the Society; cattle, horses, farming appliances, etc.   The funds realized from these, timber and
personal property sales, were available for the discharge of the
debts of the Society, the costs of the division of the property
and proposed later dissolution of the corporation.   A cash dividend was made to the members of the Society — amounting to
some $200.00 per member, with the understanding that another
dividend would probably be made when the timber notes were
paid and all final expenses provided for.   The farm lands were
apportioned into the requisite number of lots according to the
appraised value of respective sections.   That is, had the land
been uniform in value each distributee would have received some
fifty odd acres.   But as the land varied greatly in its fertility,
accessibility, etc., the survey, appraisal and division produced al-

---

[25] See deed of realty on pp. 90–92.   The commissioners chosen were
not members of the Society.

lotments of unequal number of acres, but supposed equality of value. Each member got an equal amount of cash and a section of farm land and a home or property in the village. The hotel, for instance, represented several shares and was assigned to the landlord and the members of his family entitled to a share each. The allotments were assigned by the Commissioners. The members of the Society had no choice. They were bound to accept what was apportioned to them. The natural plan was followed as far as practicable, of assigning to each the property, or a portion of it, which he had occupied or employed in his vocation; the mill to the miller; his shop to the blacksmith, the garden to the florist, and so on.

On September 29, 1898, the deed, by the Society of Separatists of Zoar, (incorporated) in whose title the lands stood, to the various individual distributees was signed and acknowledged at Zoar and on October 13, 1898, it was recorded in the Recorder's office, New Philadelphia, Tuscarawas county, Ohio. This interesting document by which all pieces of property were granted and received in one deed, is set out in full in the latter part of this article.

The exact value of the property which each recipient member (136 in all) obtained, cannot be given. Several members informed me it would be in the vicinity of $2,500. Taking the entire Zoar (Society) population (222) and averaging the aggregate wealth, it approximates $1,500 per capita. This represents the net result of three generations of communistic labor and thrift. The average wealth per capita in the United States is now regarded as not less than $1,000. It is left to the student of sociology to speculate upon the problem whether Zoar communism paid its members (financially) or not.

This action of distribution of course annulled and abolished the communistic feature of the Society. The municipal incorporation of the village and the incorporated Society of Zoar remain intact.[26] The latter incorporation will continue until all the financial affairs of the Society are adjusted, and all litigation is

[26] At the date of this article, July 1899.

at an end.[27]   The stockholders have merely divided and come into possession, separately and personally, of what was common property.   The legal form of the corporation yet exists, its affairs not having been completely closed up.   There are still obligations to meet and claims to collect.   The apportionment of the corporate property was the withdrawal and appropriation in name and title by the individual members of the Society of their undivided and undetermined personal shares.   When all further necessary details are arranged the corporate organization, as such, will be legally dissolved and the Separatist Society of Zoar will be no more.

AFTER VIEW OF ZOAR.

In the summer of 1899 the writer made a second visit to Zoar with the purpose of observing how the good Zoarites were getting on under the new dispensation.   "Mine host" of old still ran the hotel and the first evidence of the new era was the telephone closet in the hall with long distance telephone facilities.   Zoar was now on the electric current, in instant touch with all the world.   Near by on the wall hung a tutti-frutti chewing gum slot machine.   Surely Zoar was fully up to date.   Opposite the hotel, across the street, was an ice cream parlor in full, though not very brisk, blast.   It was difficult to imagine the staid and sober Zoarites eating ice cream and chewing gum, but they were.   The village had taken on a new and modern aspect.   The streets had been named.   The houses had, in many cases, been repaired and more or less renovated.   The roofs had been renewed and here and there slate roofs had superseded the antique tiles or the moss grown shingles.   Several dwellings

---

[27] After the distribution of the property suit was brought in the courts of Tuscarawas county, against the incorporated Society of Zoar, by a former member (Mrs. Paulina Beiter), a great granddaughter of the original Bimeler, for a distributive share.   Other ex-members set up claims in cross-petitions.   The legal claim was that as the Society had been declared, in previous suits, not a perpetuity, then the dissolution of the Society worked a reversion of the property to its original holders and they or their heirs were entitled to recognition.   This suit was lost, by the claimants, in the Common Pleas and Circuit Courts.   It is not known whether it will be carried to the Supreme Court of the State.

had donned new chimneys of bright yellow brick. On the side street near the hotel, was a brand new modern frame dwelling, the first, and thus far the only one in town, built in modern style and plan and with a basement furnace, which was a novelty to the natives. Without doubt, as the street phrase is, Zoar "was getting a move on itself." Even domestic life was rapidly assuming phases of our most advanced city civilization, for since the change from communism, and for the first time in all the history of Zoar, a divorce had been applied for by both partners after a life-long sharing of joys and sorrows. The Doctor had deserted his old quarters and built a spruce little convenient two room office. Even his drugs and bottles were new and so was his practice, in manner and in field. "No pent up Utica contracted his powers" now, his skill extended to the farmers for miles around and he was continually "on the go." A card and revolving hand in the window indicated his absence and the hour of his return. The good doctor himself seemed to have renewed his youth and taken a fresh start in his profession.

The former quarters of the genial shoemaker and his assistants were occupied as dwelling rooms, and it was rumored that a foreign brewer was negotiating for the building for a "sample room." The cheery master cobbler had established himself in the ancient log church which dated back to the early years of the colony, and was probably the oldest structure in the village, and for many years had been used as storage room. He told me one of his two assistants had abandoned the leather bench for the farmer's plow. The other "help hand" had opened a new and rival establishment. It was the first, and indeed, the only case of competition ever experienced in Zoar.

"There's hardly enough for two shops," the shoemaker said, "but I guess I'll find something to do," he added in a serious tone that sounded like a refrain of regret over the "sure support" days gone by. The machinist was surveying his somewhat the "worse for wear" plant, and to my inquiry if all (Zoarites) were now happy, he replied cautiously, "Some, not all." I did not press the question but the manner of his answer led to the inference that he belonged to the "not all" class. The miller was emphatic in his approval of the "new way." With energy and enthusiasm he had improved the mill, put in several hundred dollars in repairs and modern machinery and exultantly showed me the "finest flour in the market." An hour or so before breakfast I strolled into the blacksmith shop and found the stalwart smithy pumping the bellows with one giant bare arm and with the other holding a horseshoe, with long nippers, in the glowing forge. "Well, how do you take the new deal?" He hesitated a moment, then jabbed the iron rather vigorously in the hot coals and said, "O, pretty well; I'm my own boss now but I have to work harder."

"Is everybody pleased?"

"Some was satisfied and some was 'kicking' a little," he replied in terse but slang terms. The huge horse stables, cow stable and sheep stable were like great banquet halls deserted. At the entrance of the cow stable mending the whippletree of "his" wagon was my old friend the jester and "boss" of the mustered out, milk brigade. He greeted me cheerily and to the invariable inquiry said, "Well, I like it pretty good but I have to work just as much as before. No, I got not the whole stable, dere was six shares in the stable, I gets one and my home and some farm. The farm was pretty fair but I likes to sell out and go away."

"You don't have a hundred cows to look after now?"

"No, everybody has der own cow or buys de milk already, Yes, you bet, dey all has to hustle now, dat was sure."

His desire to sell and get away was not exceptional. There were several such, particularly among those who had no specific employment and were suddenly thrown upon their newly acquired farms for a living. Very few of them had been trained in any craft or trade and those who had mostly worked upon the farm lands had done so in a mechanical or even menial manner, under guidance and direction and with learning but little knowledge of the science or principles of agriculture. This was a weakness of the communistic system. The paternalism in the government was a hindrance to thinking as well as to acting for oneself.

> "For just experience tells, in every soil,
>   That those that think must govern those that toil."

It had made children of men and women. It would be difficult if not quite impossible for the older ones to "pull up stakes" and move away. Some of them, not equal to the labors of the field, proposed to rent their farms or have them worked on shares. A few of the younger ones had already left the village to seek their fortunes elsewhere. In some cases the new regime had brought back a wandering one. My former barber no longer presided at the chair, but in his stead was installed a young man of similar age. He proved to be a Zoarite who, not content with the prospects of the future, had left home a few years before and plied his trade in the large cities. He had returned now to look after his old father and mother, whom the new *status* had thrown upon their own exertions. "I thought they would need me, now," he said with filial affection, and no doubt they would. He was sorry he had left, as, if he had remained, he could have come in for a "divy", as he expressed it. The former barber dropped in while we were talking. He was above age at the time of the distribution, but had not previously become a full member of the Society, though born and raised in it. He was, however, acknowledged as a probationist member and received his share, like some others, on account of his semi- but legally recognized relation to the community.

One of the most significant indications of the return by the relieved people to the normal conditions of life was the keen sense of delight and pride with which they used the possessive pronoun and spoke of their "own" possessions.

"Is that your house?" I asked two or three, and with a contented expression that would fairly beam they would utter the possessive "mine." The baker and his wife had hung over the door the sign "Bakery," and had converted their front room into a sale shop with counters and cases, the latter filled with cookies and pies, tidily displayed to tempt the appetite. As a fellow visitor and myself stood upon the porch the husband of the woman drove up with a new buggy and dapper horse. "Where did your husband get that fine rig?" I shall never forget the tone of self-satisfaction with which she promptly replied, — "That is OURS — we bought it. Isn't it nice to have your own horse?" This innate propensity for personal proprietorship is

a factor in human nature that the advocate of universal communism fails to properly appreciate or consider.   Some power will
have to mould over mankind before it will yield the desire to
possess the earth or at least as much of it as he can earn or inherit.   As Josh Billings has philosophically remarked, "there is
still a great deal of human nature in mankind."

The survey, appraisal and successful distribution of the
property was a delicate and difficult work.   There were so many
parties to be satisfied and such a diversity in the nature of the
property to be divided.   Much praise is due the commissioners,
Messrs. Foltz, Fisher and Becker; the Society's attorneys, Messrs.
Neely and Patrick; the trustees of the Society, Joseph Breymaier,
Christian Ruof, Sr., and John Bimeler, and more than to any
other one, Mr. Louis Zimmerman, the Secretary and Treasurer
of the Society.[28]

The grounds and buildings of the brick church were reserved
in the apportionment of the realty and set aside to the village
corporation for the public use.   But now a grave and singular
question arose.   There was no church organization.[29]   To whom
or what organization should the church property be devoted?
Ministers of some of the leading denominations, both Evan-
gelical and otherwise, sought to invade the community and secure

----

[28] Mr. Louis Zimmermann was assistant secretary and treasurer of the
Society from 1882 to 1889 and secretary and treasurer from the latter date
to the present time.   He has therefore had practically the control and management of the commercial and financial interests of the Society for some
seventeen years.   In that position and particularly in the work of closing
up the affairs of the Society, he has displayed marked ability and tact.   All
classes in the Society had implicit confidence in his honesty of purpose,
wisdom of action and his fidelity to the duties entrusted to him.   His grand-
father, Louis F. Birk, was one of the original Zoar emigrants of 1817.   Mr.
Zimmerman was thoroughly loyal to the Zoar Society and its aims and work,
so long as it could be successful, but was one of the first forced to the conclusion that the time had arrived to abandon the communistic plan.   Mr.
Zimmerman was for many years the manager of the general retail store
of Zoar and at the distribution he and Mr. August Kuecherer received, besides other property, the store as their portion.   Joseph Bimeler is also as-
sociated in the management of this store.

[29] It has been stated to the writer that the Separatists, as a religious
sect, no longer exist in the old country.

for their respective sects the field apparently left open for some missionary influence. Several of the ex-Zoarites, if that expression may be permitted, highly resented the imputation that they were subjects for "conversion," or that they were fallow ground for orthodox spiritual seed. As one of the members said to me, "I don't see why we are not as good as some of the people who want to regenerate us." "But," said another, "we must have some kind of a religious organization and after awhile some of us will get together and form a church society."[30]

---

[30] In 1876 William Alfred Hinds visited the Zoar community and gave a very interesting account of the religious phase of the village life at that time. We quote from his conversation with one of the oldest members. Jacob Ackerman was then acting as the religious leader, he having been selected to that informal and rather nondescript office by the Society. Hinds asked:

"Did Ackerman, your present leader, directly succeed Baumeler, your first leader?"

"No. Baumeler died August 27, 1853. As his successor we unanimously appointed Jacob Sylvan—a good writer, but no speaker. Christian Weebel read his discourses for him. After Sylvan's death, October 13, 1862, Weebel took the spiritual lead; but the majority of the members were not fully satisfied, and in 1871 Jacob Ackerman was appointed, he being the oldest trustee, and having labored hard for the Society. We desired to honor him."

"What peculiar ceremonies have you?"

"None at all."

"How do you regard the Bible?"

"We believe in both the Old and New Testament, and in Christ as the Savior of the world."

"What great objects have you as a Community?"

"Our object is to get into heaven, and help others to get there."

"Do you expect your system will sometime be generally accepted?"

"I formerly believed it would spread all over the world. I thought every body would come into Communistic relations. I believe so still, but I don't know how far our particular system will prevail. In heaven there is only Communism, and why should it not be our aim to prepare ourselves in this world for the society we are sure to enter there? If we can get rid of our wilfulness and selfishness here, there is so much done for heaven."

"That is a good point, certainly; but haven't you confidence in the perpetuity of your Community?"

"I will not undertake to decide the question of its perpetuity. If God wishes to have it continued He will see that it is done."

BIMELER'S EFFECTIVE INFLUENCE.

A study of the constitution of the Society impresses one with the ability and astuteness displayed in its provisions. It confers the rights of equality and universal democracy upon the members of the community while at the same time it deftly, and to a cautious degree, institutes a "one man" power. This latter feature is embodied in Article III, creating the office and defining the scope of the authority of an "Agent General." This unique public function was contrived solely for the benefit, and as far

---

"Joseph Baumeler was a remarkable man, I judge?"

"Yes; when he was our leader we knew everything would come out all right. He had the superintendence of our business, and he was at the same time our preacher, and cared for the spiritual interest of the Community. He was also our physician. He was, indeed, a remarkable man."

Jacob Ackerman is so sincere that he frankly admits that he is a little discouraged about the future of Zoar—discouraged because the younger generation do not come under the same earnestness that controlled the original members. They fall into the fashions and ways of the world, and will not brook the restraints that religious Communism requires. The unfavorable condition of Zoar in this respect may well excite reflection. Evidently it is not enough that a Community had a religious afflatus and intelligent, earnest men at its beginning. It must find means to keep that afflatus alive and strong, and to replace its founders, as occasion requires, with men of equal intelligence and earnestness; and to this end *ordinances* become of great value.

The ordinances of the Zoar Community are few and weak. They have nothing answering to mutual criticism, and no meetings except on Sunday, and these are not generally attended, and are not of a kind to elicit special interest or enthusiasm. I was present at one of them. Not more than one-third of the members were there. The women sat on one side, the men on the other, both facing the desk, from which Jacob Ackerman read one of the discourses of Baumeler. The reading was preceded and followed by the singing of a hymn, with the accompaniment of a small organ. No one except Ackerman said a word; and he confined himself entirely to reading. There is no meeting, I was informed, in which all take part—where all hearts flow together in unity and devotion. Is it any wonder that the young people stay away, and that they lose their attraction for Community life? A Community should be an enlarged home, differing from the small home only in its increased attractions and its greater facilities for improving character." Hinds' American Communities, pg. 29, et seq.

as it might be such, for the aggrandisement, of Joseph M. Bimeler. By Article I, regulating elections, it will be observed, that the Agent General was to be elected, "unlimited in term, as long as he possessed the confidence of the Society." But this Consul for Life seems nowhere to have attempted to improve or abuse the Napoleonic opportunity entrusted to him. Bimeler was a most remarkable character. He must have been possessed not only of unusual acumen but invincible probity. In a wider field and under more favorable circumstances he might have become a great and a national leader. It is to be seriously regretted that more is not now known of his origin, early life and personal incidents of his career. I failed to learn the date or place of his birth or whether he came from Württemberg, Bavaria or Baden, as all those sections of Germany contributed members to the original (1817) emigration. It is claimed that Bimeler was not primarily the protagonist of the communistic scheme for the Zoarites but that his fellow settlers in the pioneer home discerning his elements of popular premiership, advocated the community of property and equality of person in order to forestall his superiority and their subordination.[81]

As we have previously noted in this article, the emigrants settled in primitive huts and cabins as separate families. Any surplus earnings, saved above their needs, were to be applied to the purchase of a proportionate division of the land, held by Bimeler in trust. But they made little headway. The poorer, the older and the feeble could not hold their own. After two years of this unequal struggle, several of the shrewder members, who were jealous or fearful of Bimeler's growing supremacy, proposed a common proprietorship. They urged this plan upon the necessity of protecting the infirm and the indigent. This project was not original or new to the proposers. They had the example of the "Harmonists" before them. Bimeler, it is said, reluctantly yielded to the communists. But once committed to it, he was its soul and mind, the "guiding spirit of all their enterprises." And it is to his indefatigable labors and

---

[81] History of Tuscarawas County, published by Werner, Beers & Co., Chicago, 1884.

well directed efforts, it must be acknowledged, the Society was indebted for its growth and prosperity.

Bimeler is attributed with no greater ambition than the desire to have his fellow countrymen comfortably settled in their new habitation, freed from debt and enjoying all the benefits of "the land of the free and the home of the brave." He was bound to his people with ties of deep and sincere sympathy. He was the head of a great family, — and his guidance was a patriarchal one. He was the first and only pastor of the Society, and conducted its religious services during his life time. In this respect, as we have shown, he had no successor and the religious life as well as the financial growth of the commuity culminated under Bimeler's administration.[32] He was not only their spiritual guide and adviser and agent in all temporal things, but he was also "their physician to heal their bodily infirmities." He controlled and managed everything.[33] Certainly we have record of few men so complete in character, so rounded in attainments and so versatile in talent. He is credited with great social qualities and while austere and decisive when dealing with his people as occasion required, he nevertheless was genial and hospitable.[34]

---

[32] They are tenants in common, and each member of the Community thinks of advancing his own interest only by furthering that of the whole. They are called to a particular stand every morning, and to each are assigned their respective labors for the day, by their director. Their perfect harmony of feeling, unity of interest, simplicity of manner, universal frugality and untiring industry, directed by an able financier, have enriched the whole, and have brought their premises into the highest state of cultivation.

Jenkins' Ohio Gazetteer (1837), pg. 491.

[33] Bimeler was the main engine; he had to do all the thinking, preaching and pulling the rest along. While he had strength all went on seemingly very well; but as his strength began to fail the whole concern went on slowly. I arrived the week after his death. The members looked like a flock of sheep who had lost their shepherd. Bimeler appointed a well–meaning man for his successor, but as he was not Bimeler, he could not put his engine before the train. Every member pushed forward or pulled back just as he thought proper; and their thinking was a poor affair, as they were not used to it.

Noyes' History of American Socialisms, pg. 136.

[34] Henry Howe's visit to Zoar, 1846, related in Howe's History of Ohio.

AN OLD HOME.

He won their affection as well as their respect. One tradition is that he acquired his position of influence and superiority by his gentle manner and tender solicitude and kindness to the sick on the vessel during the voyage to America. But the better belief is that he was agreed upon as their Moses before they left their Fatherland, for it is known that he was a recognized teacher and leader among the German Separatists previous to their departure.

We have alluded to the comfortable, if not rather luxurious, mode of life indulged in by Bimeler. Aside from that there nowhere appears any evidence of his taking any advantage of his prestige. That he was incorruptibly honest is universally acknowledged. He had unquestioned full control of the commercial affairs of the Society and no charge of mismanagement, much less misappropriation, was ever brought against him. He held in his own name the title of all the property of the Society. The trusteeship was not set forth in Haga's deed to Bimeler but ten days before his death, by will, he acknowledged the trust and bequeathed it all to the "Society of the Separatists of Zoar."[35] The will and testament of Mr. Bimeler is a model document and we herewith insert it in full:

I, JOSEPH MICHAEL BIMELER, of Zoar, Tuscarawas County, and State of Ohio, being weak in body, but of sound and disposing mind, memory and understanding, do make and publish this as my last will and testament. That is to say: I give and bequeath all my property, real, personal, and mixed, of whatever kind, be the same in lands, tenements, trust or otherwise, bonds, notes, claims book accounts, or other evidences of debt of whatever nature, to the Society of Separatists of Zoar, and its assigns, forever; hereby declaring that all the property I ever held, real and personal, within the county of Tuscarawas, has been the property of said Society, and was held by me in trust for said Society, to which I now return it.

And I do hereby appoint John G. Grozinger, Jacob Silvan and Jacob Ackerman, trustees of said Society, as my executors, to carry this, my last will, into effect.

In testimony whereof, I have hereunto set my hand and affixed my seal, this sixteenth day of August, A. D. one thousand eight hundred and fifty-three.

[SEAL.]   JOSEPH M. BIMELER.

---

[35] Michener's Annals of Ohio, p. 326.

6

SIGNED, sealed and declared by the above named J. M. Bimeler, as his last will and testament, in presence of us (the words "and its assigns forever", interlined before signing).

JACOB BLICKENSDERFER,
JOSEPH C. HANCE.

In personal appearance Bimeler is described as unprepossessing. "He was physically imperfect, one of his eyes was much larger and more prominent than the other," and as already stated, he was lame and walked with difficulty. I sought diligently for some picture or portrait of Bimeler, but was informed none was ever known to exist. He was averse to being reproduced in "living colors on the glowing canvas," probably for obvious reasons. We have reverted again to Bimeler's characteristics that he may be accorded just position in the history of Zoar. Unquestionably his strong personality was the main force that held the Society together and impelled it to the zenith of its career. There was no one to fill his place; indeed, had his equal been found to succeed him, it is doubtful if the Society could still have prospered or even continued unabated.[36] The internal conditions were no longer the same and the external influences were different and decidedly adverse.

Thus reads the recital of "the strange, eventful history" of the Zoar community. The beautiful little berg, "loveliest village of the plain," has burst the bonds of its seclusion and—in the phrase of the day—joined the procession of American progress. It could not stem the tide of conventional civilization. What its future may be, time alone will disclose. Surely there can be no one who has seen or known those simple and true-hearted people that will not grant them the hearty wish of Rip Van Winkle — "May they live long and prosper."

CONCLUSION.

From the days when philosopher Plato wrote his ideal *Republic* (400 B. C.) down to More's *Utopia* (1516 A. D.) and

---

[36] The facts of the history of the principal Communistic Societies of the United States "teach that in proportion as a community loses the afflatus of its first leaders and relies upon doctrines and the machinery of governments, it tends to death; in other words, a community needs, for its growth and progress in all stages of its career, a living power at its center not inferior to that which it had in the beginning." Hinds' American Communities, p. 153.

on to the latest scheme, Bellamy's Equality, the political thinker and sympathetic socialist has ever exercised the utmost powers of his imagination to conceive of a perfected state of society in which all shall be equal in rights, privileges, possessions and enjoyments. America has been a fruitful field for such experiments. Twice in our later social history have there been epidemics in communism — revivals in socialistic experiments, viz: in 1824, when Robert Owen visited this country and through the ardent advocacy of his views attracted a large following known as "Owenites." Many efforts were made to practically carry out his delusive doctrines. Those efforts were all shortlived and financially disastrous. Again in 1840 the teachings of the French Fourier (1772-1837) were popularly promulgated in the United States and encouraged by many distinguished American scholars and writers. American Fourierism is particularly interesting from the intellectual and literary coloring it received. That picturesque and grotesque association for "agriculture and education," the famous Brook Farm (1842) in which our most brilliant *litterateurs* participated, was one of the conspicuous products of the Fourier movement.

It has been stated that beginning with the Jamestown colony (1607), down to the latest one of note, that of Ruskin, Tennessee (1894), some three hundred communistic societies, in various phases, have been attempted in the United States. Their average life has been about five years and there are alive to-day perhaps twenty-five, mostly leading a precarious existence. The delightful dream of Bellamy has experienced many rude awakenings. The plucky little Society of Zoar has run its course and fought the good fight. Their simple record is one of earnest endeavor and honest toil. The chronicler of the times should not fail to faithfully recount their deeds and write on memory's tablet the description of those Zoar days when the peaceful villagers,

> "Far from the madding crowd's ignoble strife,
>   Their sober wishes never learned to stray;
> Along the cool sequestered vale of life,
>   They kept the noiseless tenor of their way."

LEGAL DOCUMENTS.

We should regard this article incomplete unless accompanied by the documents herewith appended. They mostly speak for themselves. The articles of Association of April 1819 and the amended articles of March 1824 have already been given on pages 7-10 ante.

ARTICLES OF INCORPORATION.

TO INCORPORATE THE SOCIETY OF SEPARATISTS OF ZOAR, TUSCARAWAS COUNTY.

SECTION 1. *Be it enacted by the General Assembly of the State of Ohio,* That Joseph M. Bimeler, John G. Grosinger, Jacob Syfong, Michael Fetters, Christopher Plotz, John George Lepold, Solomon Sala, George Aukerman, Jacob Walz, Christian Hanzler, John Neff, Lewis Buck, Philip Sell, George Ruff, Godfrey Kapple, Christian Weible, Conrad Lebold, John C. Fetter, John Miller and John Fogle, and their associates be, and they are hereby created a body politic and corporate, by the name of "The Society of Separatists of Zoar," with perpetual succession; and by their corporate name, may contract and be contracted with, sue and be sued, plead and be impleaded, defend and be defended, in all courts of all and equity, in this State and elsewhere; may have a common seal, which they may break, alter, or renew at pleasure; shall be capable of holding property, real, personal and mixed; either by purchase, gift, grant, devise or legacy; and may sell, alien, dispose of and convey the same; and the property and other concerns of the corporation, shall be under the management and control of Trustees appointed for that purpose; and said corporation shall have power to form a constitution and adopt by-laws for its government; to prescribe the number and title of its officers; and define their several powers and duties; to prescribe the manner in which members may be admitted and dismissed; and all other powers necessary for its corporate concerns: *Provided,* That said constitution, by-laws, rules and regulations be consistent with the constitution and laws of the United States and this State; and *Provided,* also, that the clear annual income of said Society shall not exceed one thousand dollars.

SECTION 2. That the persons named in the first section of this act, or any three of them, may call a meeting of the society, by giving ten days' notice thereof, by advertisement set up at the place of public worship in the village of Zoar, for the purpose of forming a constitution and adopting by-laws for the government of said society, and of doing such other business as may be necessary for the efficient management of said corporation.

SECTION 3. That the members of said society, or such number of them, as by said laws shall be necessary, shall meet annually on the second Tuesday of May, at the place of holding public worship, for the purpose of electing officers of said corporation.

SECTION 4. That any future Legislature may amend or repeal this act: *Provided,* such amendment or repeal shall not affect the title of any real or personal estate, acquired or conveyed under its provisions, or divert the same to any other purpose than that originally intended.

W. B. HUBBARD,
Speaker of the House of Representatives.

WM. DOHERTY,
Speaker of the Senate.

February 6th, 1802.

AMENDED ARTICLES OF INCORPORATION.

An Act to amend the act entitled, "An act to incorporate the Society of Separatists of Zoar, in Tuscarawas County.

SECTION 1. *Be it enacted by the General Assembly of the state of Ohio,* That so much of the second section of the act entitled, "An act to incorporate the Society of Separatists of Zoar, Tuscarawas County," passed February sixth, one thousand, eight hundred and thirty–two, as limits the clear annual income of said society to one thousand dollars, be and the same is hereby repealed; and the society are hereby authorized to receive a clear annual income of any sum not exceeding ten thousand dollars.

SECTION 2. That if said society, for any cause, shall not elect officers on the day specified in said act, then any five members of the society may order an election by giving at least ten days' notice by posting up printed or written notices of the time and place of holding such election in three of the most public places in the village of Zoar, one of which shall be at the place of holding public worship.

SECTION 3. The fourth section of the act, to which this is an amendment, be and the same is hereby repealed.

SECTION 4. This act shall take effect from and after its passage.

ELIAS F. DRAKE,
Speaker of the House of Representatives.

SEABURY FORD,
Speaker of the Senate.

February 21, 1846.

ARTICLES OF AGREEMENT SIGNED BY THOSE BECOMING MEMBERS OF THE FIRST OR PROBATIONARY CLASS.

We, the undersigned, members of the first class of Separatists, party of the first part, and George Gasely, Jacob Ackerman and Christian Ruof, trustees elect, and their successors in office, of the Separatists' Society of Zoar, in the County of Tuscarawas, and State of Ohio, party of the second part, have, through confidence mutually reposed in one another, established and by these presents do establish the following rules and principles of social compact for the better fulfillment of the duties of mankind, which we owe to one another, and also for the furtherance of our spiritual and temporal welfare and happiness.

ARTICLE I.

We, the said party of the first part, do declare, that by our own free will and accord we have agreed and by these presents do agree and bind ourselves to labor, obey and execute all the orders of said trustees and their successors in office; and from the day of the date hereof henceforth to use all our industry and skill in behalf of the exclusive benefit and welfare of the said Separatists' Society of Zoar, and continue to do so, as long as strength and health will permit, to the entire satisfaction of the said trustees and their successors in office.

ARTICLE II.

And we do also hereby agree and bind ourselves firmly by these present, to put our minor children under the care and control of the said trustees and their successors in office, in the same manner as if they had been bound by indentures to serve and dwell with them and their successors in office, for and during the term of their minority, subject to all the duties and likewise entitled to the same rights and protection as indentured children by law are subject and entitled to, until they shall have attained their proper age as defined by the statutes of the State of Ohio.

ARTICLE III.

And the said trustees do hereby for themselves and their successors in office, agree and bind themselves to furnish the said party of the first part with suitable dwelling, board and clothing, free of cost, the clothing to consist at any time of not less than two suits, including the clothes brought by the said party of the first part to this society; and in case of sickness, necessary care and attendance is hereby promised to the said party of the first part; and this performance of the trustees and their successors in office shall be considered by the party of the first part a full compensation for all their labors and services, done either by themselves or their minor children, without any further claim or demands whatever.

ARTICLE IV.

Good and moral behavior, such as is enjoined by strict observance to the principles of Holy Writ, are by both parties hereby promised to be observed; hence, it is clearly understood that all profane language, immoral words and acts, which may cause offense amongst the other members of this community, are not only wholly to be avoided, but, on the contrary, all are to endeavor to set good examples and to cherish general and mutual love.

ARTICLE V.

The object of this agreement being, furthermore, to preserve peace and unity, and as such can only be maintained by a general equality among its members, it is, therefore, severally understood and declared that no extra demands shall be made or allowed in respect to meat, drink, clothing, dwellings, etc. (cases of sickness excepted), but such, if any can be allowed to exist, may and shall be obtained by individuals through means of their own and never out of the common fund.

ARTICLE VI.

All moneys, which the said party of the first part either now possesses or hereafter may receive into their possession, shall without delay be deposited in the common fund of this society, for which a receipt, payable on demand, is to be given; but upon the request of said party of the first part, in order to procure extra necessaries, as the case may be, a part or the whole of said deposit shall be refunded to the owner.

ARTICLE VII.

All manner of misunderstanding and differences shall be settled by way of arbitration and not otherwise; that is, by a body of three or five persons, to be chosen by both parties, and their decision shall be binding on both parties.

ARTICLE VIII.

All rules and regulations contained in the foregoing articles (if any there be which are not plain enough or are subject to misapprehension) shall be so understood as never to be in opposition to but always in perfect accordance with the morals, usages, principles and regulations of the members of the second class of the Separatists' Society of Zoar.

ARTICLE IX.

These articles being fully and fairly understood, to their strict and faithful performance, both parties bind themselves in the most solemn manner, jointly and severally, their children, heirs, executors, administrators and successors in office by the penal sum of fifty dollars, current money of the United States of America.

ARTICLE X.

If, in consequence of the foregoing, a penalty upon any one of the parties to this agreement shall be laid, then, in case of refusal or non–compliance, the party so refusing may be prosecuted for the same before any magistrate or justice of the peace in the township, county and state wherein the defendant may reside, and judgment may be had agreeable to the laws of this state; and said magistrate or justice of the peace shall forthwith proceed to collect such penalty and pay it over to the party who, by law, is entitled to the same. In testimony whereof, both parties have hereunto set their hands and seals this 14th day of October, in the year of our Lord 1833.

TRANSLATION OF THE CONSTITUTION OF THE SEPARATIST SOCIETY OF ZOAR.

INTRODUCTION

TO THE CONSTITUTION OF THE SEPARATIST SOCIETY OF ZOAR.

Pursuant to an act of the Legislature of the State of Ohio, passed A. D. 1832, No. 126, entitled: "An Act to Incorporate the Society of Separatists of Zoar, Tuscarawas, County, Ohio," we, the undersigned members of said Separatist Society of Zoar and its vicinity have found it expedient to renovate our hitherto existing Constitution, as contained in the following articles:

In the name of God the Father, and Jesus Christ, the Son, and the Holy Ghost, Amen.

In order furthermore to secure to our consciences that satisfaction, proceeding from the faithful execution of those duties which the Christian religion demands, and to plant and establish the Spirit of Love as the bond of Peace and Unity for a permanent foundation of social order for ourselves and our posterity forever, we, therefore, seek and desire, in accordance to pure Christian principles, to unite our various individual interests into one common stock and conformably with the example of the Primitive Christians, all inequalities and distinctions of rank and fortune shall be abolished from amongst us, and, consequently, to live as brethren and sisters of one common family.

Pursuant to the foregoing principle and resolution, we, voluntarily, unite and bind ourselves by this joint agreement, under the name and title of Separatist Society of Zoar. And we obligate ourselves, each to the other, that we will hold to the following articles and rules, that we will observe and support the same to the best of our abilities, which from the day of the date thereof, shall be in force and virtue in law:

ARTICLE I.

REGULATING ELECTIONS.

All elections, for the divers necessary officers of the Society, shall, agreeable with the provisions of the act of incorporation, be held on the second Tuesday of May, annually, and in accordance with the statute of the State of Ohio, be decided by ballot and majority of votes. On said election day shall annually be elected one Trustee (extraordinary circumstances excepted); annually, one member to the Standing Committee; quadrennially one Cashier, and one Agent General unlimited in term, as long as he possesseth the confidence of the Society.

The time and place, when and where the election shall be holden, also the number and kind of officers to be elected, shall be made known by the Trustees of the Society, at least twenty days previous to the election, for which purpose the Society, or any ten members thereof, shall, at each election, appoint a committee of four persons whose duty it shall be to conduct the election in conformity to the laws of this country.

The Society shall elect all its officers from amongst the members thereof, whereby special reference shall be had to the necessary and requisite qualifications, integrity and faithfulness of the candidates.

ARTICLE II.

ELECTION OF TRUSTEES AND THEIR DUTIES.

The Society shall elect from amongst its members three suitable persons as its Directors or Trustees, and their successors in office, who shall take charge of the joint property of all undersigned members. Said Trustees shall, as stated in the first article, be elected by majority and agreeable to the following regulations: The majority for three years; second majority for two years, and third majority for one year, and after the expiration of one year, annually one Trustee. Should the case occur, that two or more candidates of one and the same office receive an equal number of votes, then the balloting shall be repeated, until a legal majority be obtained. Each Trustee may remain in office for three years in succession unless circumstances to the contrary, such as death, sickness, absence, refusing to serve, etc., render such impossible; or in case the misconduct of any one of said Trustees cause the Society to discharge one or the other, and to fill such vacancy, as said Society may choose, which right of discharging and replacing, the said Society reserves itself, before the expiration of the ordinary term of three years, or even of one year. Yet, each Trustee shall remain so long in office, until his successor be chosen.

Said Trustees are hereby empowered and in duty bound to take charge of all the property, real and personal, which this Society, either now or in the future, may possess, including all property of newly accepted members, movable and immovable, of whatever name and description it may be; likewise are they authorized to receive all kinds of legacies, donations and personal claims, in fine every species of property to which any one of the members may at any time have just claim, to demand and collect the same by legal proceedings, and shall appropriate and apply the same conscientiously to the best of their knowledge and skill, in behalf and for the exclusive benefit, use and advantage of said Society. And it shall also be the duty of said Trustees, carefully to furnish each member, without respect to person, with board, clothing and dwelling and other necessaries, alike in days of sickness and of health, as good as circumstances will allow. Said Trustees shall furthermore take charge of the economical affairs of this Society, to consult over and direct all the business, and consequently to assign to each individual member its duty and work to be performed, to which at least the majority of said Trustees, if not all of them, shall be agreed. Said Trustees are hereby empowered to appoint sub-trustees or agents, as many and to whatever purposes they may see proper and necessary, and all such sub-trustees or agents shall be responsible to the said Trustees for all their transactions. Said Trustees shall fill the different branches of economy with suitable persons, who shall conduct the same subject to the control of said Trustees, and liable to like responsibility for the conduction thereof as other sub-trustees or agents. But all resolutions in regard to important undertakings shall be submitted to and subject to the approbation of the Standing Committee, and said Trustees shall at all times be responsible for all their transactions to said Standing Committee. Casual discord, differences and misunderstandings, shall throughout, by way of arbitration, be settled amicably by the Trustees of said Society. In case that this cannot be accomplished by and through said Trustees, then the court of arbitration or appeal, cited in subsequent articles, shall solely decide.

As the said Trustees are, by this article, bound to maintain and promote peace and order in the Society, they are furthermore hereby authorized to propose to the board of arbitration or standing committee such regulations and improvements calculated to facilitate those purposes, and if a majority of both bodies approve of the measures thus proposed, as proper and necessary, they shall thereupon be recommended to be observed as such, provided that such amendments be in no wise contradictory to these articles.

ARTICLE III.

ELECTION AND DUTIES OF THE AGENT GENERAL.

In order, partly to simplify, and likewise in many instances to ease the business and duties of the Trustees, the Society shall elect an Agent General who shall act for and in the name of said Society. He is hereby authorized to buy and to sell, make and conclude contracts, and to discontinue or annul them again; to employ agents beyond the circle of the Society, and to correspond with them; also to issue, and again to accept orders; to direct and to superintend, to the welfare of the Society, all its trading and commercial concerns; in fine, all affairs, which, in any wise appertain to the aforesaid line of business, of whatever name, shape and description they may be, shall be carried on under his direction and superintendence. In like manner shall all the manufactures and similar works be under his superintending care, to the furtherance and improvement of which he shall pay due regard and so regulate them in such a way and manner, as he shall from time to time find it most conducive to the general good of said Society.

The Agent General shall furthermore be entitled to appoint sub-agents, when and as many as he shall stand in need of, who shall be empowered to transact, in his name, all such business as he shall see proper to charge them with, and said sub-agents shall be held responsible to the Agent General for all their transactions. And said Agent General shall, in appointing sub-agents, act by and with the consent of the Trustees, whose concurrence shall also be necessary in all undertakings of moment and importance. And for the due administration of the powers and duties hereby committed to his care and charge, he shall be accountable to the Standing Committee of the Society.

All deeds, mortgages and similar instruments of writing shall be executed in the name of the Trustees, and be placed to the safekeeping of the Agent General.

ARTICLE IV.

ELECTION AND DUTIES OF THE STANDING COMMITTEE.

By virtue of these articles the Society shall elect from amongst its members a Standing Committee, which shall consist of five persons, but in case a vacancy of one or two members thereof should occur, either by death, sickness, absence or otherwise, then the three remaining members shall be capable of transacting business, until the next succeeding election. This committee shall be invested with the concentrated power of said Society, and shall execute all those duties which are marked out for it in this constitution. In all extraordinary cases shall this Standing Committee serve as a Court of Appeal, and shall, as the highest tribunal, be hereby empowered, to decide as such, and the judgment thereof shall be final and binding in all cases, provided, that no complaint shall be brought before it for decision, except by way of appeal, that is, in case one or both of the contending parties should be dissatisfied with the decision of the Trustees. Trustees can never at the same time be members of this committee. The election of said committee shall be so regulated that annually one member to said committee shall be elected, and that each member hold the office for five years successively, and are at all times eligible again, as long as they possess the confidence of said Society.

ARTICLE V.

ELECTION OF THE CASHIER AND HIS DUTIES.

The Society shall choose a Cashier or Treasurer, to be elected for the term of four years, and shall after the expiration of such term be eligible again, as long as the Society entrust him with the station. Said Cashier shall take charge of, and duly administer to all its financial concerns, and beside him none of the members shall be entitled to hold any money without order from the Cashier; even the Trustees and the Agent General shall deliver up all monies, notes, bonds, checks, etc., as belonging to the Society, into the treasury without delay, and every transgressor of this provision shall by any member or person whosoever, be prosecuted for the same before the Trustees of the Society, and shall be treated by them according to the provisions of the tenth article.

It shall also be the duty of the Cashier to appropriate and apply all monies received, conformably to the direction of the Trustees, the Agent General and the Standing Committee, exclusively to the benefit of the Society; to pay the Society's debts; defray its general necessaries, and to credit said Trustees with the surplus fund. All and every person who have charge over any one or more of the branches of economy, shall hand in their accounts to the Cashier at such time as he shall see proper to order the same. And the Trustees are hereby entitled to request from the Cashier an annual account of his transactions, if they deem it necessary.

The Cashier shall have the right, if circumstances require it, to appoint a clerk to keep regular records of elections, and of such other important measures, which the divers officers shall deem necessary.

ARTICLE VI.

DELIVERY OF PROPERTY, AND DUTIES OF THE MEMBERS.

We, the undersigned, members second class of the Separatist Society of Zoar, declare by these presents, that all our property, of all and every description, which we either now or in future may possess, movable or immovable, or both; together with all claims, titles, rights, devise and legacies, etc., of whatever kind and name they may be, as well for our own selves, as our descendants, heirs, executors and administrators, shall be forever given up to said Society, with the express condition, that such property shall, from the date of the signature of each member, forever henceforth, consequently after the death of each respective member, be and remain the exclusive property of said Society. Also do we promise and bind ourselves, most faithfully and industriously to execute all the orders and regulations of said Trustees and their sub-trustees or agents, without opposition and murmuring; and we likewise agree to apply all our strength, good will, industry and skill, for life, to the general benefit of said Society, and to the satisfaction of its Trustees. Likewise do we promise and agree, under the same conditions and regulations, to place our children, whilst they are in a state of minority, under the directions and regulations of said Trustees, in same manner, as if they were legally bounden by lawful indenture, to them and their successors in office, until they shall have attained their proper age, as defined by the laws of this State.

ARTICLE VII.

ACCEPTANCE OF MEMBERS.

In accepting new members, the following rule and order is to be observed: Each and every person wishing and desiring to become a member of the second class of this Society shall first of all have attained to the lawful age, that is, a male person shall be twenty-one and a female eighteen years of age; secondly, shall such person or persons have lived in, and dwelled with the Society, for the term of at least one year, and shall have been a member of the first class, of this Society, (without exception, if even born and educated in the Society) and provided, that they have faithfully fulfilled the contract, previously concluded with the Trustees of this Society at their entrance into the first class. If such person or persons can show forth the aforementioned qualifications, and the resolution not being prematurely made, but who, by their own free will and accord, self-convinced, are so resolved, such person or persons, shall make known their intention to one or more of the Trustees, whose duty it shall be to hear such person or persons, and if, after having taken the applicant's motives into consideration, no well-founded causes for rejection or postponement be found, then said Trustees shall make it known to the Society at least thirty days previous, and appoint the time and place, when and where such signing shall be performed; and if, during such interval no complaints or objections from the part of the Society, or any of its individual members against such person or persons be made, thereupon they may be admitted to the signing of this constitution, and after signing such, are thereby constituted members of the second class of the Society and shall be considered and treated as such; provided, that, in case such new member shall have kept secret any of its contracted debts or other obligations, foreign to the Society, such member shall have forfeited all privileges and rights of membership, in case sufficient proof be found to establish the fact.

ARTICLE VIII.

EDUCATION INSTITUTE.

In accordance with this article the Society shall keep or establish a general education institute for all the children in the community, at the head of which such male or female overseers shall be placed, whose qualifications shall be found best suited for said purpose. And agreeable to this proviso, all the parents of children in this Society, bind themselves by these presents, to deliver up and place their children, after having arrived at the third year of their age, or sooner, to the overseers of said institution, where such children shall receive, according to their age and faculties, appropriate education and tuition. Said overseers shall be chosen and engaged by the Standing Committee, subject to the express duty, that they shall exert their best endeavors and care to give those children, placed under their care, as well in moral as physical consideration, the best possible education, thereby having in view, not only the attainments of scientific branches of knowledge, but also gradually to train them to performing the divers branches of manual labor. And it is hereby made the duty of said committee to keep a strict superintendence over this institution; and they shall also be authorized to place such children, as soon as their age, abilities and bodily constitution will permit, under the control of the Trustees, who shall give them such employment, as they may be able to perform.

ARTICLE IX.

POWER OF THE TRUSTEES TO COLLECT AND TAKE CHARGE OF HERITAGES, ETC.

This article authorizeth and empowereth the Trustees and their successors in office, in the name of the Society, to hold and take possession of all remaining property of deceased members, with all their rights, titles and claims whatsoever, to demand, or cause the same to be demanded and collected; and finally, they are hereby invested, as the universal heirs in the name of the Society, to act with full right and power, as if such deceased person or persons were yet living, themselves demanded and acquitted for the same; hence, the children, friends and relatives, whether they be in or without the Society, can not be or become heirs to such an heritage of a deceased member, since all property forever is, and shall remain the portion of said Society. And the Trustees of said Society are, and shall be hereby authorized to empower other suitable persons in or out of the Society, to demand and collect, or cause to be demanded and collected, monies, estates and effects of persons either yet living or deceased, in same manner, as if such person or persons, for whom such was done, had themselves demanded and collected the same, received it and receipted therefor.

ARTICLE X.

CONTENTIONS, ETC.

Casual contentions between two or more members, and complaints of whatever kind and description they may be, shall be brought before the Trustees and by them to be examined and settled. But, in case one or the other party should not be satisfied with the decision of said Trustees, or should any one or more of the Trustees themselves be envolved in such contentions, etc, then appeal may be had to the Standing Committee or Court of Appeal, whose decisions shall in all cases be final and binding; whosoever shall act contrary to this provision, and will not be satisfied with their judgment looseth and debarreth him or herself of all further enjoyments and rights of a member.

ARTICLE XI.

SECEDING MEMBERS.

Should any member or members find cause to secede from the Society, they shall make known such their intentions to one or more of the Trustees, whose duty it shall be to notify the Society thereof, in order that if any complaints be existing against such member or members, they may betimes brought forward to said Trustees, who shall thenceforward act in respect to them agreeable to all the attending circumstances. But should any seceding member or members, unknowingly to the Trustees, have contracted any debt or debts upon the community, or been the cause of subjecting the Society to any costs or injury, in such case said member or members shall make satisfactory restitution, or otherwise render such indemnification as the said Trustees shall demand, and in case such seceder or seceders should not content themselves with the judgment of said Trustees and refuse to make such satisfactory restitution, in that case both parties, the Trustees and seceding members, shall be entitled to an appeal to the Standing Committee, and the decision thereof shall in all cases be binding and final. Should any person or persons, notwithstanding this provision, be dissatisfied, and apply to a court of justice beyond the limits of the Society for assistance, in such case they are also hereby bound to render due indemnification for all damages and loss of time thereby caused to and sustained by said Society.

In case any seceding person should refuse to comply with the demands of the Trustees, in pursuance of the decision of the Standing Committee, the Trustees shall be authorized to prosecute such person or persons, and by course of law to bring them, or cause them to be brought to the due fulfillment of the duty or payment as aforesaid. Furthermore shall the committee be authorized to act in like manner with all those, who can account of acting contrary to duty and good order, have been expelled from the Society, to expunge their names and signatures, and to excommunicate them from all further enjoyment and right of a member of this Society. Neither the seceding persons, who leave the Society of their own accord, nor those who are expelled therefrom, can ever, by virtue of their signatures, and by the provisions of this article, under no pretense whatever, in no wise, make any demand or claim, either upon property brought to the Society, or for their labor, or any other services, which they may have rendered the Society, in whatever the same shall have consisted, notwithstanding; yet such person or persons may, if they choose, submit such their pretensions to the Standing Committee, whose opinion shall decide, whether or not, or under what condition such applicants shall be entitled to receive any indemnity.

All judgments of the committee, issued pursuant to the foregoing prescriptions, shall be made out in writing and recorded in a book to be kept for that purpose, which shall in all courts of law and equity be considered as valid and incontestable. Each given judgment of said committee shall be handed over to one or more of the Trustees, by virtue of which he or they are authorized to execute such judgment, or cause it to be executed, either on voluntary terms, or by the ordinary process of law.

This constitution shall never, in any wise, be broken or annulled by dissatisfied or seceding members.

ARTICLE XII.

CONCERNING THE CONSTITUTION.

The Society can at any time, whenever deemed expedient and necessary, alter this their constitution, or any one of the articles thereof, or add thereto, provided, that such alteration or addition shall always be founded upon the principles of Unity and Conservation of the Society, and only then practicable if at least two-thirds of all the members be in favor of it. In no wise shall this present renewed constitution ever be viewed as declaring or representing ineffectual and void the articles signed by the members on the fifteenth day of April, 1819, and those of the fifteenth day of March, A. D. 1824; on the contrary, said articles shall be acknowledged as the basis to this present constitution.

All unintelligibleness, equivocation, or deficiency, which, peradventure, might exist in this constitution, shall always be construed and treated in favor of the Society, and never to the advantage of individual members.

At least annually, at a suitable time, shall this constitution be publicly read at the place of public meeting.

Written and concluded in Zoar, Tuscarawas county, State of Ohio, the fourteenth day of May, in the year of our Lord one thousand eight hundred and thirty and three.

HARVEST SCENE.

INCORPORATION OF THE VILLAGE OF ZOAR.

To the Honorable, *the Board of Commissioners of the County of Tus-carawas, and State of Ohio:*

The undersigned householders, resident in the Town of Żoar, Tus-carawas county, Ohio, respectfully ask the following territory with the village of Zoar as its center, be incorporated and be known and designated as the incorporated Village of Zoar, to–wit: Beginning in the middle of the E. line of the 4th qr. of Tp. 10 in Range 2 of the U. S. Military lands, thence W. on a line parallel with the S. line of said qr., Tp. 400 rods to the middle thereof, thence N. by a line parallel with the E. line of said qr. Tp. 400 rods to the middle of the N. line of said qr. Tp., crossing said line and continuing N. in the same direction 80 rods to a point, thence E. on a parallel line with the N. line of said qr. Tp. 560 rods, to the S. W. corner of 40 acres, belonging to the estate of D. K. Nixon, in the N. half of Sec. 15 in Tp. 10 and Range 1, thence due S. through lands of the Zoar Society, by a parallel line with the W. line of said Sec. 480 — to the road leading from John Bayley's farm to Zoar, thence W. in the said road and crossing the road leading from Zoar Station to Zoar, and also crossing the Tuscarawas river, in the same direction 160 rods to the place of beginning. The proposed number of inhabitants residing in the proposed corporation is about three hundred and twenty (320). The petitioners hereby appoint Simon Beiter as their agent.

JACOB ACKERMANN, SR.,	JOHN GROETZINGER,
JOHN G. RUOF,	SAMUEL RICKER,
SAMUEL HARR,	LEVI BIMELER,
CLEMENS BREIL,	JACOB BREYMAIER,
ANDREW GOUTENBEM,	DAVID BEUTER,
CHRISTIAN RUOF,	LORENZ FRITZ,
OBED RUOF,	FREDERICK BREIL,
LOUIS ZIMMERMAN,	SOLOMON BREIL,
SIMON BEITER, SR.,	JULIUS NOTTER,
JACOB BURKHART,	JONATHAN BENTER,
ANTON BURKHART,	BENJAMIN RICKER,
GOTTLIEB SEIZ,	SIMON BEITER, JR.,
SEBASTIAN BURKHART,	JACOB KUEMMERLE,
JOSEPH BREYMAIER,	JOHN RICKER,
AUGUST NEUMANN,	CHRISTIAN HOYH,
JAKOB RICKER,	JOHN RUOF,
CHARLES ZIMMERMAN,	CHARLES BREIL,
EDWARD BEUTER,	WILLIAM KAPPEL,
CHRISTIAN ACKERMANN,	WM. EHLERS,
CHRISTIAN J. RUOF, JR.,	MICHAEL MUELLER,
JOHN BREYMAIER,	HENRY EHLERS,

7

David Breymaier,	Franz Strobel,
John Notter,	Jakob Buehler,
Bainard Beuter,	August Kuecherer,
Burnhart Beiter,	William Kuecherer,
John Kuecherer,	John Beiter,
John Sturm,	Levi Beiter,
John C. Breymaier,	Mathias Dischinger,
Benjamin Beiter,	Leo. Kern,
Jacob Ackermann, Jr.,	Charles Kappel.
John D. Bimeler,	

Notice is hereby given that a petition praying for the incorporation of the Village of Zoar, and adjacent territory, as a village, has been presented· to the Commissioners of Tuscarawas county, Ohio, and that the same will be for hearing on Wednesday, May 7th, 1884.

Simon Beiter, *Agent.*

Mar. 13 W. 4.

The State of Ohio, $\Big\}$ ss:
  Tuscarawas County,

I, Addison M. Marsh, being duly sworn say that the notice here-unto attached was published in the *Tuscarawas Advocate,* on the 13th day of March, A. D. 1884, and continued therein four consecutive weeks, during all of which time said newspaper was printed and in general circulation in said county.

Addison M. Marsh, *Publisher.*

Sworn to and subscribed before me this 5th day of June, 1884.

P. S. Olmstead, *J. P.*

Printer's fees, $2.50.

Commissioners Journal, Tuscarawas county, Ohio, Wednesday, March 5th, 1884. In the matter of the Incorporation of the Village of Zoar, the Petition of Jacob Ackerman, Sr., and sixty other citizens of said village having this day been, by their agent, Simon Beiter, filed with the Board of Commissioners for Tuscarawas county, Ohio, praying for the incorporation of said village, under the name and style of the Incorporated Village of Zoar, together with an accurate plat of the territory sought to be incorporated, and it appearing to said Board that the matter of said petition was proper to be set out therein, thereupon on said day it being at a regular session, said Commissioners caused said petition, together with the attending plat to be filed in the office of the County

Auditor, and ordered that the time and place of hearing on said petition, should be Wednesday, May 7th, 1884, at 10 o'clock A. M., and at the Auditor's office of said county, in New Philadelphia, Ohio, Simon Beiter, agent, was then and there notified of said time and place of hearing, Wednesday, May 7th, 1884. In the matter of the petition of Jacob Ackerman, Sr., and sixty others, for the incorporation of the village of Zoar, for hearing on this day, the same is postponed until Tuesday, June 3d, 1884, and leave granted to petitioners to amend petition. Tuesday, June 3d, 1884. In the matter of the incorporation of the Village of Zoar, hearing on which application was adjourned to, this day came Simon Beiter, agent for said 'village and on leave hereintofore granted, filed amended petition, Map and Plat of Territory described therein. This matter came on for hearing in said amended petition, whereupon the Board find that said petition contains all the matter required, that its statements are true, that the name proposed is appropriate, that the limits of the proposed incorporation are accurately described and are not unreasonably large or small, that the plat is an accurate Plat of the Territory sought to be incorporated, that the persons, whose names are subscribed to the petition are electors residing on the Territory, that notice has been given as required of the hearing on this application, and that there is the requisite population for the proposed incorporation. Therefore it is ordered by the Board of Commissioners for Tuscarawas county, Ohio, that the prayer of the petitioners be granted and that the village of Zoar be and hereby is established an Incorporated Village under the name and style of the "Incorporated Village of Zoar."

H. B. HEFFER,

SAM'L RUFER,

WM. E. LASH,

Commissioners of Tuscarawas County, Ohio.

Filed with the Secretary of State, August 25, 1884.

DEED OF THE PROPERTY BY THE TRUSTEES TO THE MEMBERS ON THE SEPARATION OF THE SOCIETY.

This deed, the result of the division of the realty belonging to the Society, is an unique document. The entire distribution of the property into the respective shares is embraced in one deed by the trustees of the Society to the grantees—the recipient members of the dissolving Society. By the permission of the County Surveyor, Mr. George E. Hayward, the plat showing the respective allotments, both in the village and the farm land to each member, is published and accompanies this volume. The village cemetery, church and school properties were reserved public possessions for the village.—E. O. R.

Deed of the Distributed Realty.

The Society of Separatists of Zoar
        to
    Carl Ehlers, et. al.

Know all men by these presents that whereas we, Carl Ehlers, Louisa M. Ehlers, Charles J. Breymaier, Otelle Bimeler, Peter Bimeler, Mary Bimeler, Ernestine Breil, Mary Breil, Charles Breil, Clemens Breil, Flora Burkhart, Christian Ruof, Jr., Matilda Ruof, Conrad Breymaier, Charlotte Breymaier, Jacob Breymaier, Caroline Breymaier, Caroline Kuemmerle, Levi Beuter, Caroline Beuter, Jonathan Beuter, Pauline Beuter, Gottlieb Seitz, Anna Seitz, Pauline Kuecherer, Albert Kuecherer, Selma Ruof, Jacob Kuemerle, Johana Kuemerle, Rosina Roth, Barbara Wetter, Jacob Buehler, Joseph Buehler, Thersie Buehler, Levi Bimeler, Caroline Bimeler, Anton Burkhart, Salome Burkhart, Bertha Kuecherer, Rudolph Ruckstuhl, Sarah Ruckstuhl, Simon Beuter, Jacob Burkhart, Emilie Burkhart, Frank Ackerman, Louisa Ackerman, Jacob Ricker, Lydia Ricker, Joseph Beuter, Caroline Beuter, Bernhart Beiter, Mary Beiter, Albert Beuter, Alma Beuter, John Beiter, Elizabeth Beuter, Sebastian Burkhart, Regina Burkhart, Leo Kern, Sabina Kern, Geo. Ackerman, Wilhelmine Ackerman, David Beuter, Amanda Beuter, Elizabeth Ricker, Anna Maria Peterman, Joseph Bimeler, Amelia Bimeler, Mathias Dischinger, Jacobine Dischinger, Jacob Dischinger William Kappel, Wilhelmina Kappel, Simon Beuter, Jr., Rosena Beuter, Christian Hoyh, Mary Hoyh, Joseph Breymaier, Bertha Breymaier, Jacob Ackerman, Mary Ackerman, Josephine Ackerman, Elizabeth Mock, Christian Ruof, Mary Ruof, Benjamin Beuter, Salome Beuter, Charles Kappel, Wilhelmine Kappel, Jacob J. Sturm, Ellen S. Sturm, John Ruof, Caroline Ruof, John Groetzinger, Lea Groetzinger, Regina Breymaier, Elizabeth Fritz, John Ackerman, Charles Zimmerman, John Sturm, August Kuecherer, Barbara Kuecherer, C. F. Sylvan, Lydia Sylvan, John Bimeler, Louisa Bimeler, Mary Sylvan, Rosina Harr, Ella Rieker, Louisa Zimmerman, Louis Zimmerman, Antoniette Zimmerman, Julius Notter, Rebecca Notter, Andreas Gauterbein, Louisa Gauterbein, Christiana Strobel, John Kuecherer, Rosena Kuecherer, Lawrence Kuecherer, Emelia Burkhart, Obed Ruof, Eliza Beiter, Emma Heid, Lillian Ruof, Josephine Ruof, Hattie Ackerman, Edwin Breil, William Kuemerle, John Buehler, John Ricker, Orthoford Kappel and August Kuecherer, Jr., members of the second class of the Society of Separatists of Zoar, all of the County of Tuscarawas and State of Ohio, and the only living members of said second class, on the 10th day of March, A. D. 1898, together with Christian Ackerman and Frederick Breil, both of whom have since died, entered into a written contract of that date as between ourselves, the said Christian Ackerman and Frederick Breil and the Society of Separatists of Zoar, a corporation, provided among other things for the partition and division among us and the said Christian Ackerman and Frederick Breil of all the real estate of said The Society of Separatists of Zoar, with the exception of certain reservations specifically set forth in said written contract, the legal title to all of said real estate was then and still is in the name of the said The Society of Separatists of Zoar, and held by it in trust for us and said two deceased members and their respective heirs, and which said written contract is of record in the minute book of the said Society on page 30 to 48 both inclusive, which book is in the office of said Society in the village of Zoar in said county, and in the custody of Louis Zimmerman, as Treasurer of said Society, reference to which record is hereby made.

And whereas by the terms and provisions of said written contract, We, together with the two deceased members, selected and appointed Samuel Foltz, Henry S. Fisher and William Becker Commissioners to make said partition and division and to designate in their report and statement by numbers and on a plat to be prepared by George E. Hayward, the surveyor selected by us and said two deceased members, the parts and portions of said real estate which each of us is to receive as our respective shares and allotments and the respective shares and allotments of each of said two deceased members.

And whereas the said commissioners have fully performed their duties required of them by the terms of said written agreement and have made their statement and report in writing and had said plat prepared as required by the terms of said contract, and which statement and report is in the words and figures following and is the original statement and report, to–wit:

We, the duly selected and authorized Commissioners for the purpose of sub–dividing, allotting and apportioning the lands (and appurtenances thereto belonging) of the Society of Separatists of Zoar, Ohio, designated to us for that purpose, do hereby make the following report of our findings and action in said division and allotment and declare that to the best of our ability and judgment we have made an equitable, just and impartial partition and allotment of the real estate of said Society submitted to us for that purpose.

In making such division it has been with the idea, first to make a complete appraisement and invoice of all said real estate without reference to persons or location.

The appraisement being conducted by personal visits to all tracts in question, the boundaries and limits being duly designated by us and afterward surveyed, computed and compiled by the surveyor.

After arriving at the result and sum total the partition was conducted with a view to giving so far as practicable, village property, agricultural lands and timber lands to each of the parties in interest severally or jointly when so requested.

Authorized Report of Division Commissioners.

We met and organized May 2, 1898, and the work of appraisement began May 12, 1898. Geo. E. Hayward acted as our clerk throughout the work.

Following the terms of the signed contract we do hereby certify that we, in conjunction with the duly authorized and appointed surveyor, Geo. E. Hayward, have gone over the land allotted and have found it to be in accordance with our wishes, and we approve of the returns of said surveyor as shown by monuments and the plat of the land, and we have personally inspected this report and find that it shows the result of our action and that the work of the Clerk is hereby approved.

(Following this are the divisions and allotments, by metes and bounds, which are omitted here as being not pertinent to the purpose of this document.—E. O. R.)

SAM'L FOLTZ,
WM. BECKER,
HENRY S. FISHER.
Division Commissioners.

Signed Sept. 1, 1898, at Zoar, Ohio.

GEO. E. HAYWARD, *Clerk.*

And whereas by the terms and provisions of said written contract we and each of us, and each of said deceased members, covenanted and agreed one with the other and each one with all the others, that we and the said Christian Ackerman and Frederick Breil would accept the allotments and parcels of said real estate which should be set apart to us respectively by the said commissioners as our respective shares of the whole from which said allotments should be made, and that each of us would then by a proper deed of conveyance executed and delivered, release all our respective rights, title and interest and estate to each of the others of us in and to the respective allotments and parcels set apart to us respectively and would do and perform all things necessary on our respective parts to make good title to the respective owners of said allotments and parcels. Now, therefore, we and each of us in consideration of said written contract and for the purpose of fully carrying out its provisions in regard to said real estate on our respective parts as well as in consideration of the sum of one dollar to each of us in hand paid by each of the others of us, the receipt of which is hereby acknowledged, do hereby demise, release and forever quit claim to each other and to their respective heirs and assigns forever, all our right, title and interest and estate, legal and equitable, in and to the several parcels and allotments designated by numbers to each of us respectively in the said statement and report of the said Commissioners, and designated by the same numbers and by our respective names on the parcels allotted to us respectively upon the said plat of said allotment of said lands, a copy of which plat is hereto attached and made a part and parecl of this deed of conveyance, and said original plat will be found on the plat records of said Tuscarawas County, each of us excepting and reserving our respective right, title, interest and estate in and to the parcels and allotments so designated in said statement and report and on said plat to each of us.

In witness whereof we and each of us have subscribed our names this 20th day of September, A. D. 1898.

(Signatures following next omitted).

(Certificate of Acknowledgment follows here).

And whereas the said The Society of Separatists of Zoar, a corporation organized under the laws of the State of Ohio, and named in the foregoing deed of conveyance of the members of the second class of the said The Society of Separatists of Zoar, by John ·Bimeler, Joseph Breymaier and Christian Ruof, its duly elected and qualified Trustees, being duly authorized and empowered thereto by a resolution entered in the minute book and journal of the said Society on the 10th day of March, A. D. 1898, for and on behalf of the said The Society of Separatists of Zoar, executed the written contract mentioned in said foregoing deed of conveyance, reference to which is hereby made, whereby they covenanted and agreed with all the members of the second class of the said The Society of Separatists of Zoar, named in the foregoing deed of conveyance, that they would when the division and allotments provided for in said written contract should have been made and accepted by said members, by proper deed or deeds convey the legal title to each of said parcels and allotments to the respective parties to whom the same should be awarded by the commissioners named in said written agreement.

And whereas the said Commissioners have made their statement and report in writing and have in said written report designated by consecutive numbers the parts, parcels and allotments awarded by them to the members of the second class respectively, who are now living, and to the respective heirs of Christian Ackerman and Frederick Breil, two of said members of the second class who have died intestate, leaving heirs since they signed said written contract and have caused to be prepared by George E. Hayward, the surveyor selected and appointed by the said members of the second class, by the terms of said written contract a plat of said division and allotment on which is designated by the same numbers and the respective names of the said several members of the second class the parts and portions of said real estate awarded to each of said living members and to the heirs of the said two deceased members, and showing by said numbers and names the parts and portions awarded to some of said members jointly and the others thereof severally, which written report and statement of said commissioners is incorporated into and is a part of the said foregoing deed of said members and is hereby made a part of this deed of conveyance, and a copy of said plat is attached to and made a part of said foregoing deed and is hereby made part and parcel of this deed of conveyance, and the second of which plat will be found in plat records of said Tuscarawas County, and whereas the said living members and each of them have accepted their respective portions and allotments as designated in the said commissioners report and on said plat as aforesaid, and have executed and delivered their foregoing deed of release as between themselves and have fully complied with the terms of said written contract on their part to be performed in respect to the division of said real estate.

Now, therefore, in consideration of the foregoing premises and for the purpose of carrying into effect the terms and provisions of the aforesaid written contract, as well as in consideration of the sum of one hundred dollars to it in hand paid and the receipt whereof is hereby acknowledged, the said The Society of Separatists of Zoar, has bargained and sold and does hereby grant, bargain, sell and convey unto the said ...... (Names omitted here) and their heirs and assigns forever the several parts and parcels and allotments of said real estate set apart to them respectively by the commissioners and designated and described by them in their said report, and designated and described by their numbers and names on said copy of said plat as aforesaid and on their respective parts, parcels and allotments as aforesaid, together with all the appurtenances, rights, privileges and easements thereunto belonging or in any wise appertaining.

To have and to hold the same to said living members respectively and and to their respective heirs and assigns forever, either jointly or severally, as they appear in the said report of said Commissioners and on said copy of said plat.

In Testimony Whereof the said grantor, the said The Society of Separatists of Zoar, by John Bimeler, Joseph Breymaier and Christian Ruof, its Trustees, has caused its signature to be hereunto subscribed and its corporate seal to be hereto affixed this 20th day of September, A. D. 1898.

THE SOCIETY OF SEPARATISTS OF ZOAR,

Executed and delivered in our presence.

By JOHN BIMELER,

MRS. KATE HAYWARD,   [Seal]   JOSEPH BREYMAIER,
JAMES G. PATRICK.   CHRISTIAN RUOF,
Trustees.

THE STATE OF OHIO,
TUSCARAWAS COUNTY, } ss:

Before me a Notary Public in and for said County personally appeared the above named John Bimeler, Joseph Breymaier and Christian Ruof, the Trustees of the above named The Society of Separatists of Zoar, and acknowledged the signing and sealing with the corporate seal of the said The Society of Separatists of Zoar, of the foregoing conveyance to be their voluntary official act and deed as the Trustees of said corporation and the voluntary corporate act and deed of the said The Society of Separatists of Zoar.

In Testimony Whereof I hereunto subscribe my official signature and affix my official seal this 20th day of September, A. D. 1898.

(Stamps, $182.00, cancelled.)

JAMES G. PATRICK,

[Seal] *Notary Public.*

Received October 10, 1898 at 10 A. M.
Recorded October 13, 1898.

M. SCHNEIDER, *Recorder.*